Beliefs
and
Values

Beliefs
and
Values

Karl E. Scheibe

Wesleyan University

HOLT, RINEHART AND WINSTON, INC.

New York   Chicago   San Francisco   Atlanta
Dallas   Montreal   Toronto   London   Sydney

PREFACE

To STUDY PSYCHOLOGY requires ambition. As an outgrowth of physiology and philosophy, modern psychology has inherited the technical complexity of the former and the conceptual perplexity of the latter. Furthermore, the several redefinitions of psychology in the last hundred years have not made the study of this subject easier. The twentieth century has, for example, seen the rejection of "soul" and "consciousness" as appropriate objects of psychological inquiry and the adoption of the principle that the proper business of psychology is to study the behavior of living organisms. This is hardly a modest aim.

Mind is a concept that bridges the transition from the old "soul" psychology to modern behavioral psychology. Because behaviorism, *mind* referred to a substance or a place, whereas now it is a collective name for a set of behaviorally related *processes* for which the adjective "mental" seems appropriate. While the early behaviorists preferred a completely mindless psychology, modern psychologists are hard at work studying mental processes such as how one solves problems, makes choices, or constructs plans.[1] But they have learned well to avoid the crystal-gazing sort of mental study that has no relation to what the organism is doing. The

---

[1] The rewelcoming of terms cast out by the early behaviorists was noted by D. O. Hebb in his 1960 Presidential Address to the American Psychological Association: "Mind and consciousness, sensation and perception, feelings and emotions, all are . . . properly part of a behavioristic psychology" (Hebb, 1960, p. 741).

scope of psychology is broader now than it was when the prime subject was "experience" and when the methods were those of contemplation and disputation. But progress is more possible with the enlarged definition of psychology as the study of behavior.

However, progress can be achieved only if one forgets (at least temporarily) the overwhelming problem of accounting for *all* behavior and focuses on the possibility of understanding *some kinds* of behavior of *some kinds* of organisms. Most contemporary psychologists are willing to leave the task of achieving an overall synthesis of the "Laws of Behavior" to the indefinite future. It seems challenge enough for the present to worry about limited behavioral problems—language and communication, sexual behavior, perceptual discrimination, or social influence. One such limited problem area is denoted by the term *beliefs and values*.

From this present work the reader can expect several features, the first being that I consider it pertinent to speak of beliefs and values only as they relate to a behavioral context. A related premise is that the words "belief" and "value" are drawn from the idiom of specifically *human* thought and action. Hence, little direct reference will be made to studies of other animals. (It is not illegitimate, however, to talk as though some other animals had beliefs and values, and in some instances comparative applications will seem quite obvious, if incidental.) This suggests another expectation the reader should have about the present essay. To wit, beliefs and values have a limited range of convenience in psychological theory. The aim is to define this range of convenience with a minimum of stretching, and with no attempt to be all-inclusive. This is an ambitious endeavor, leaving no small field.

Many realms of human activity may be analyzed in these terms of beliefs and values. Religion, besides comprising abstract doctrine and creed, is a great behavioral force in the life of man.[2] Men *do* things—they offer themselves as martyrs or hunt witches—because of religious convictions combined with social circumstances.[3] And while it may be an

---

[2] "Depending upon the socio-religious group to which a person belongs, the probabilities are increased or decreased, for example, that he will enjoy his occupation, indulge in installment buying, save to achieve objectives for the future, vote Republican, favor the welfare state, oppose racial integration in the schools, migrate to another community, develop a commitment to the principle of intellectual autonomy, have a large family, complete a given unit of education, or rise in the class system" (Cline & Richards, 1965, p. 570; after Lenski, 1961).

[3] That such occurrences are not merely historical curiosities is attested by the self-immolation of several Buddhist monks during the Vietnamese war. Witch-hunts are also with us. An item from a South American newspaper of December 13, 1967 reports as follows (my translation from the Portuguese): "Angry neighbors unleashed a witch-hunt in Sincelejo (Colombia), according to police. The wrath of the neighborhood was aroused by numerous unhappy marriages attributed to love philtres (potions) prepared by witches, residents of the poor regions of the city. In view of the threats of the betrayed wives and husbands, the police decided to maintain a guard in the witches' neighborhood" (*Estado de Minas,* Belo Horizonte,

annoyance to medical science, there is convincing evidence that men are not cured by doctors alone, but on occasion by visiting some special shrine or by taking some holy potion (see Frank, 1961). Consider habitual gamblers, whose behavior does not "extinguish" even though the treatment is one of constant punishment, seemingly contradicting a principle of traditional learning theory (see Cohen & Hansel, 1956). On a collective level, men fight wars in defense of principle (higher values) or at least claim they do. The stock market rises and falls in response to mysteriously caused fluctuations in "confidence in the market," and a financial panic may, in one day, radically alter the status of an economic system without modifying in the slightest the quantity of capital goods and services within that system. The eternal popularity of prophets in human society—whether they be old-fashioned soothsayers, ancient or modern astrologers, religious leaders, scientists, newspaper columnists, or touts at the race track—is further testimony to the relevance of beliefs and values to human affairs (see Lewinsohn, 1961).

No promise is made here that all of these topics will receive satisfactory psychological clarifications, but it is claimed that the range of behaviors implied in the list has strong analytic communality. Moreover, this communality may be discerned in the behaviors of subjects in psychological laboratories—special environments, to be sure, but still part of the "real world."

This should provide a fair sampling of the prejudices from which the present work develops. Here is a confessed preoccupation with human behavior and an admission to a fascination for the bizarre things people do. Here is the expressed confidence that a psychological discussion conducted in terms of beliefs and values will be both interesting and useful to the understanding of a certain range of human behavior. Here is confidence in the continuity of the same real world, from the psychological laboratory to the market place, the psychiatrist's couch, the back ward of a mental hospital, the gambling casino, or the voodoo shrine. Reference to differences in the beliefs and values that support behavior may help account for the vast differences in what people do at these various stations.

A word is appropriate here about the organization of this book. Chapter I is an attempt to provide historical and conceptual background for the psychology of beliefs and values that is elaborated in the rest of the book. While this material is essential for understanding the relation of the present work to the rest of psychology, it may be desirable to skim

---

Brazil). Lest this be thought merely a characteristic of primitive culture, it bears noting that on the same page of this newspaper was a notice of a funeral service conducted in San Francisco, California, in which a self-professed warlock and his witch wife consigned the soul of a deceased friend to Satan and everlasting fire, because "he would not have wanted it otherwise."

Chapter I and proceed directly to the subsequent chapters. Chapter I might be read and appreciated by the student who has established a basic understanding of general psychology.

It will be obvious in the pages that follow that the most immediate intellectual stimuli for this work are the formulations of Professor T. R. Sarbin on cognitive psychology and social role theory. Less obvious, but of considerable importance, are debts to my students in courses in cognition, motivation, and social psychology at Wesleyan University, and to my wife, Wendy, and brother, Steve, each of whom read the original manuscript and made many helpful suggestions.

Karl E. Scheibe

Middletown, Connecticut
November 1969

CONTENTS

Beliefs
and
Values

I

Historical and Conceptual Background

It is astonishing what havoc is wrought in psychology by admitting at the outset apparently innocent suppositions, that nevertheless contain a flaw. The bad consequences develop themselves later on, and are irremediable, being woven through the whole texture of the work.   **William James**

*J*AMES'S OBSERVATION, made about 80 years ago, probably accounts for the proliferation of psychological theories. Another small theoretical fabric will be woven here, and another apparently innocent—but certainly flawed—supposition wrought quite thoroughly into the work. The importance of a psychology of beliefs and values depends upon the extent to which this particular supposition can be usefully applied—and the ability of the entire fabric to cover a variety of observations. The supposition is as follows:

What a person does (his behavior) depends upon what he wants (his values) and what he considers to be true or likely (his beliefs) about himself and the world (his psychological ecology).

Many familiar sayings in psychology are similar. Examples are "stimuli produce responses," "behavior is a function of the person and his environment," and "the state of the organism is a product of heredity and environment." These statements, including the one preferred here, are not meant to be true or false in the ordinary sense, and hence shouldn't be considered mutually contradictory. If the physicist says that man is basically "matter in motion" and the biologist that man is fundamentally a "group of living cells," an argument may seem to be imminent, especially if a psychologist then adds that all of man's scientific activity is dependent

1

upon his "mental capacities."[1] But it is obvious that the offending statements aren't intended as universal maxims. Rather, they are meant to be simply organizational guides—ways of opening a discussion of a limited set of topics.

The preference here for a formulation of behavior in terms of beliefs and values is not based upon considerations of clarity or explicitness. Neither this nor any of the traditional psychological formulas are very enlightening in themselves. But if we consider behavior to depend upon beliefs and values, we might be led to discover an interesting coherence in a wide range of observations, and to pose some promising questions for further research.

One obvious advantage of considering behavior in terms of beliefs and values is that it then becomes possible to develop applications of the formulation in terms congenial to common sense. Ordinarily, a person takes a bus (behavior) because he wants to go somewhere (value) and considers that taking a particular bus is the way to get there (belief). A person painting a tree (behavior) may seem unusual until it is understood that the objective (value) is to keep insects from invading the tree from below and that the keeper of the tree considers (believes) painting the base of the tree in a particular fashion to be an effective protection. Most human actions, such as declining to serve on a trial jury or volunteering to become a subject in a perilous experiment, can be fitted into a context of beliefs and values in such a way that they become understandable.

But insofar as a belief-value analysis is easily applied to behavior, it is also a danger, for it may stunt the development of real psychological curiosity. A man may dance to induce rain, to enjoy dancing, to please tourists, or to ward off his master's whip. The analyst of behavior cannot choose an explanation that happens to strike his fancy or one that mere verbal testimony supports. It isn't even certain that the apparent objectives of an action are in fact the values that support that action. But if it were given that the beliefs and values supporting various behaviors could be correctly identified, we would still be left with the monumental problems of explaining (a) how people come to believe what they seem to believe, (b) how they come to value what they seem to value, and (c) how the beliefs and values of one person can vary from time to time and from place to place.

The kinds of behaviors that can be accounted for in terms of beliefs and values are limited. All the runners in a race may both desire to win and have some expectation of winning. But the outcome is dependent not so much on their beliefs and values as upon differences among the runners in reaction time, muscular condition, size, oxygen metabolism,

[1] For an illustration of this possibility, see Tolman (1952).

and so on. While the problem of who wins a race may at some level be psychological, the present formulation excludes or neglects that issue. The problem for a belief-value analysis is to determine why someone decided to run a race, to write the Great American Novel, to go over Niagara Falls in a barrel, or to commit suicide. The success or failure of these ventures is not here a matter of direct concern. Some classic failures—such as the failure to turn base metal to gold or to find the fountain of youth or the philosopher's stone—can be considered from the standpoint of beliefs and values, but for this discussion it is only accidental that the world frustrates these attempts. The psychological interest comes in considering how it is that psychologically real possibilities can grow from mere wisps of information.

This touches upon one of the most fundamental and most widely accepted principles of psychology—namely, that psychological reality is not fixed and absolute but conditional and relative. This idea is expressed by psychologists of widely divergent orientations. Piaget (1955) closely documents the evolution of children's conceptions of themselves in relation to the world. Like primitive man, the very young child seems to consider himself the center of the universe; only with the accumulation of participant experience with the world does he develop a "decentered" perspective. Lewin (1936) formulated the concept of *life space* primarily to take into account the partially unique nature of the psychological environment for individuals in the same physical location. Freud (1933) suggested that through "unconscious" processes a psychological reality is constructed with such distortions as may be congenial to personal needs. Anthropological data offer innumerable illustrations of radical deviations in the way man has thought of himself and his world. Students of human personality cannot assume that "culture" is some uniform and standard developmental influence (see Honigmann, 1954).

If psychological reality is not fixed and absolute, neither is it whimsical and arbitrary. There are limits to the reinterpretability of reality. The purposes of the observer cannot occupy so large a part in determining a perspective on reality that no role is played by the outside world. Psychologists implicitly compare a person's psychological reality with some standard of objectivity to determine how rational that person is, and most frequently this amounts to a judgment of the functional consequences of looking at things in a particular way. A person may be allowed to divide humanity into saints and sinners, communists and "free men," white and black, or enemies and friends, but he will probably get into trouble if he construes men as human and inhuman (animals), terrestrial and extraterrestrial, or visible and invisible, for these distinctions have implications for action that might be considered deviant by current social conventions.

By similar logic, looking at psychological processes in terms of beliefs and values must demonstrate its own usefulness. Fortunately, the historical record provides evidence that this perspective can be interesting and productive.

BELIEFS AND VALUES IN THE HISTORY OF PSYCHOLOGY

Perhaps uniquely among the sciences, psychology has been a battleground for holy wars of words. The words used by a psychologist are tokens of his peculiar way of setting the defining problems of psychology, and differences in ways of setting these problems have been sources of acrimonious controversy. For a variety of reasons beliefs and values have not been central terms for any dominant psychology of the last hundred years.[2]

But this is not to say that the psychology of beliefs and values has no history. Indeed, its history is too extensive to be easily treated. Belief terms and value terms abound in the vocabulary of psychology. For beliefs there is the field of *cognition* and for values that of *motivation,* each a highly developed and complicated area of contemporary psychology. As conceptual units, beliefs and values have been prominent in the history of psychology, and at the present time it does not seem unnatural to use these terms as conceptual labels. Psychology has been redefined from time to time, and beliefs and values have played various parts in these new definitions.

Roots in Philosophy

Modern psychology is said to be less than a hundred years old, but more or less continuous lines of psychological thinking—if not psychological research—can be traced back to the beginnings of recorded human experience. The traditional historical endpoint for discussions of this type is Ancient Greece.

Plato, in *The Republic,* distinguished three components of the human soul, which were considered to have their own particular functions in the life of man. The functions are *knowing, wanting,* and *willing,* and the names for the corresponding faculties are *Intellect, Emotion,* and *Conation.* Plato considered that these regions of the soul develop independently. According to the differential development of the faculties, some men are dominated by their intellect, some are servants of their passions, and some spend their lives in the quest and service of power. Plato expressed a distinct preference for Intellect above the competing faculties.

[2] Cohen (1960) has noted that less than 10 percent of a sample of 60 general psychology textbooks had sections devoted to the topic of beliefs. A recent book by Rokeach (1968) entitled *Beliefs, Attitudes and Values* offers convincing documentation that this situation is changing. The book provides excellent examples of the range of empirical problems to which belief-value analyses are being applied.

This is not the place to review the philosophical issues connected with these ideas. The point is that at least since the time of Plato, men have considered knowing or believing as analytically separate from wanting or valuing. The third process, willing, has been less acceptable to subsequent thinkers as a conceptual unit and will not be discussed directly in this book.

Important subareas of philosophy correspond, if imprecisely, with the basic human processes of believing and valuing. Epistemology, or the problem of knowledge, is concerned with describing how man arrives at knowledge, and with stating criteria for evaluating the adequacy of his knowledge. Ethics is concerned with questions of value—the importance of emotions, the nature of value judgments, and standards and criteria for morality.

Of course, the concern with beliefs and the concern with values are not perfectly distinct. Plato has been often cursed for suggesting an innocent division between wanting and knowing. Obviously values have cognitive components—they must be *about* something—and beliefs have evaluative auras, especially when philosophers pronounce value judgments about them, as in the Platonic alignment of Idealism with the Intellect. Epistemologists often begin discussions of knowledge with a statement concerning its value. Aristotle affirmed that, "All men by nature desire to know."

Despite these and other complications, philosophy has maintained the distinction it first made between questions of fact and questions of value—between the questions, "What is true?" and, "What is best?" These basic questions have been appropriated by psychologists on the supposition that some scientific account might be given of how men actually function in the domain of beliefs and the domain of values. Some nineteenth century philosophic thinking directly influenced this appropriation and thus the formation of scientific psychology.

British empiricism In the latter part of the seventeenth century, John Locke formulated the basis of the theory of knowledge that was adopted by scientific psychology. Locke rejected the notion that man is born with protean ideas and held instead that experience provides the material from which all knowledge is formed.

> Let anyone examine his own thoughts and thoroughly search into his understanding and then let him tell me whether all the original *ideas* he has there are any other than of objects of his senses, or of the operations of his mind, considered as objects of his reflection. (Locke, 1965, p. 24)

Locke pictured a passive mind gathering sense impressions from the external world and from them fashioning simple ideas that might have such qualities as extent, hardness, redness, and so on. From simple ideas and continual environmental input the mind could manufacture complex ideas such as cause and effect, gratitude, and "substance."

A series of British philosophers (see Boring, 1950, Chapter 10) elaborated and developed the basic empiricist thesis. Important additions were the principles of association. The means by which ideas come to be associated are basically two—similarity and contiguity. Ideas that resemble each other tend to become bonded together in memory, as do ideas that enter consciousness in close physical or temporal sequence. Very complex notions, then, are built up associatively through the operation of these principles. The result is a vast web of ideas, corresponding in some measure to the input of basic sensations to the living organism during its history.

Associationism was adopted by the nineteenth century British utilitarian, James Mill, who in turn expounded the doctrine to his prodigious son, John Stuart Mill. The elder Mill developed associationism to the point where the idea of a house was considered to be a simple composite of the materials of which the house is built—bricks, mortar, boards, nails, and so on. The younger Mill challenged this doctrine, suggesting instead that ideas combine in a complex way that is not completely predictable—in such a way that the product is substantially different from the constituent elements. He suggested the model of chemical combination as a better analogy to the formation of ideas than the mechanical model of James Mill.

The importance to experimental psychology of the tradition of British empiricism and the doctrine of associationism is enormous. They are the sources of the great popularity of twentieth century research on associative learning. But their more immediate effect in the nineteenth century was to encourage the beginning of rigorous empirical investigations of the content of experience and of the relation of experience to physical reality.

Instincts and utilities   Positions on the question of the origin and nature of values are somewhat more difficult to describe. Any theory of human values must meet two distinct problems, conventionally called the descriptive and the normative problems. Descriptively, it must account for the existence and operation of human values; that is, it must explain why men value what they seem to value and how they express these values in actions. The normative problem is the traditional one of morality or ethics in philosophy; a theory of human values must make explicit the principles by which actions are considered morally justified.

Philosophy has produced a variety of competing normative principles. For some thinkers, ultimate justifying values are implied in the nature of God. Others (for example, Kant) assume the existence of a priori values that do not derive from God. Justification by power, or the equation of might and right, was the radical principle proposed by Nietzsche. But of more direct importance for psychology was the doctrine that the value of all actions derived from the quantity and quality of happiness they caused. This utilitarian doctrine was most ably defended by John Stuart Mill, who acquired it in more crude form from his father and his father's colleague, Jeremy Bentham.

Utilitarianism has both a descriptive and a normative form, but sometimes, as in the writings of Bentham, the distinction becomes blurred. Normatively, utilitarianism determines which of several courses of social action might produce the "greatest good for the greatest number." Descriptively, it asserts that men always act to maximize their own happiness, if only by escaping from pain or eliminating hunger or another distress. Normative and descriptive uses become blurred with the adoption of a thoroughgoing determinism. Thus, man may be considered to have no choice but to maximize his own pleasure, and the normative principle is then applied primarily to assess the wider social consequences of individual actions. But to say that behavior is directed toward increasing pleasure leaves open the question of why some actions are pleasurable and others not. The solution adopted by most nineteenth century thinkers took the form of an elaboration of a single notion, *Instinct*.

The idea of instinct as an inborn disposition to behave in a certain way under specific circumstances may be traced to the ancient Greeks, though the opposition of instinct and reason was most clearly stated by such medieval theologians as Albertus Magnus and St. Thomas Aquinas. The theological importance of instinct was that it was the animal counterpart of human reason—the accepted doctrine being that man is devoid of animal instincts. But with the publication in 1859 of Darwin's *Origin of Species* it became clear to the scientifically minded that this distinction could no longer be maintained in the same form. The distinction between reason and instinct was not destroyed, but arduous attempts were made to establish the continuity of evolution by demonstrating instinctual behavior in man and reasoning behavior in lower animals (see Beach, 1955).

Beyond reintroducing instincts to man, the theory of evolution had another profoundly important effect on theories of the origin of values. The key principle of natural selection, critical to the differentiation of life forms, supposes a range of variation in the characteristics of living members in a species. This variation, in turn, is related to the ability of individuals to reproduce themselves. Hence, it is as if there were a natural *valuation* of certain characteristics of organisms—namely, those that are functionally important in determining the number of adult organisms that could be produced from a given parent generation. Thus, the survival value of certain processes, such as sexual behavior, eating, and escaping from danger, would account for the identification of these same activities as pleasurable or productive of happiness.

In some quarters, instinct doctrine, utilitarianism, and the theory of evolution were combined to produce a new social theory. Herbert Spencer (1873) developed a theory of social evolution on these premises that confidently pointed toward eventual realization of a perfect social order, if only the natural forces of social selection could operate freely. One of the major implications was that elements of society that tend to drift toward the bottom of the social order should not be artificially supported by the more able and affluent. Welfare and charity were seen as lethal impediments to social progress.[3]

Among those who violently disagreed with Spencer was William James, who nevertheless held that the fundamental ground of all human passions and values is instinctual. Chapter III shows that among writers there was a great difference in the number and denomination of instincts attributed to man. But the ideas that basic values (a) are rooted in the nature of the beast and (b) are related to his ability to survive as a species seem to have been quite uniformly accepted when psychology was brought into the laboratory in the latter part of the nineteenth century.

Recapitulation   The intellectual background for the development of scientific psychology in the nineteenth century bore the following important characteristics:

1.   The empiricist epistemology of the British tradition was dominant. Thus, the source of ideas, knowledge, and beliefs was largely experience, and the disposition was toward analyzing experience into component parts, ideas, images, and so on. To be sure, some contemporary developments, especially in German philosophy, were markedly different; they were nativistic in epistemology and holistic as opposed to analytic in regard to the nature of experience. These tendencies influenced subsequent stages in the development of psychology.

2.   The theory of evolution, utilitarianism, and the doctrine of instincts provided the basis for questions concerning human values. Common ideas were that man has instincts, though perhaps in a more flexible and highly variegated form than animals, that man's instincts are an inherited product of his evolutionary history and hence have adaptive significance, and that the values of man therefore derive from the importance of various processes for the propagation of the species.

3.   The scientific temper of the times was greatly conditioned by the principle of causal determinism, so that even though mind was retained

[3] See Hofstadter (1955) for a thorough discussion and critique of Social Darwinism. Hofstadter shows that this social theory is an example of a perfectly good biological principle (natural selection) which is quite inappropriate when extended to the process of social evolution.

as an entity conceptually distinct from body, it was held to be subject to the same strict laws of causality.[4] Hence, the intellectual ambience of the day encouraged a strong optimism that man could become the object of his own science and could hope to render a complete account of the nature of his own experience as well as of his destiny.

The emerging form of scientific psychology was not completely determined by these conditions, for some important differences soon developed among schools of psychological thought—differences that were profoundly important for the development of a psychology of beliefs and values. Unhappily for that development, the initially dominant school of scientific psychology was all but unconcerned about beliefs and values.

German Analytic Structuralism

Wilhelm Wundt, who was trained in physiology, founded the first major laboratory of experimental psychology in Leipzig in 1879. For the remainder of the nineteenth century and for the first decade of the twentieth, this laboratory and this man virtually dominated the new mental science. A mental science it was, for the subject was consciousness or experience and the method was direct introspective observation and analysis of experience. Wundt borrowed the mental chemistry metaphor from John Stuart Mill and made it the basis for experimental research on mental processes. The philosophic inspiration of British empiricism combined with the thorough and exacting German scientific tradition to produce a thriving, if dull, offspring that came to be called structuralism.

Rarely has a scientific development been of such profound importance as a point to rebel against as was the first established experimental psychology. Part of the reason for this is inherent in the insignificance of beliefs and values in the structuralist scheme. Structuralism was not concerned with knowledge; it was not concerned with wants and motives; it was not concerned with behavior. Some would say that it really wasn't concerned with experience either, for the presupposition was always that experience could be analyzed into a small number of constituent elements, such as feelings, images, and sensation, each of which had but a few properties. The Gestalt psychologists later charged that a methodology based on these principles would necessarily destroy the holistic and uniquely organized character of conscious experience.

Thus, the importance of structuralism for the history of beliefs and values in psychology is almost wholly negative, except that structuralism

---

[4] This position is known as "psychophysical parallelism"—mind and body operating separately in a strictly parallel fashion. This was the solution to the mind-body problem provisionally adopted by late nineteenth century experimental psychology (see Boring, 1950, Chapter 9).

did, after all, bring experimental methods to psychology. If the student wants to discover why the later movements of psychoanalysis, American functionalism, and Gestalt psychology called themselves dynamic psychologies, he ought to look at the psychology of Wundt from which these movements rebelled, for the understanding will come by contrast.

American Functionalism

Structuralism was imported into the United States by psychologists educated in Germany, primarily by E. B. Titchener of Cornell University. But an important indigenous growth of American psychology was practically contemporary with German psychology, though far less conspicuous and powerful at the time.

William James is the dominant figure of early American functionalism and also perhaps the most important of all psychologists for the history of beliefs and values. While James proposed no consistent and systematic psychology of his own, he argued, with masterful eloquence, that psychology deserved something better than the treatment it was getting from the Europeans, and he greatly enlarged the scope of psychology, demanding that the science of man study man in his entirety, rather than a few relatively trivial problems.

In *Principles of Psychology,* published in 1890, James presented a list of seven topics that he considered to exhaust the problems then studied by experimental psychology. The list included, for example, "the connection of conscious states with their physical conditions" and "the analysis of space-perception into its sensational elements." It concluded with this laconic judgment:

> It must be said that in some of these fields the results have as yet borne little theoretic fruit commensurate with the great labor expended in their acquisition. But facts are facts, and if we only get enough of them they are sure to combine. (James, 1890, Vol. 1, p. 193)

It is characteristic of James that he could roundly criticize psychology without rejecting it. Indeed, he wanted to retain experience as an object of study and introspection as a method of studying it, but he was against the passivity and narrowness of the old psychology—the deadness of the post-Darwinian conception of mind. James considered man to be a live actor, with purposes he could call his own, and man's thinking to be "first and last for the sake of his doing." The knower, James stated in an essay,

> . . . is not simply a mirror floating with no foothold anywhere, and passively reflecting an order that he comes upon and finds simply existing. The knower is an actor, and coefficient of the truth on one side, whilst on the other he registers the truth which he helps to create. Men-

tal interests, hypotheses, postulates, so far as they are bases for human action—action which to a great extent transforms the world—help to *make* the truth which they declare. In other words, there belongs to mind, from its birth upward, a spontaneity, a vote. It is in the game, and not a mere looker-on; and its judgments of the should-be, its ideals, cannot be peeled off from the body of the cogitandum as if they were excrescences, or meant, at most, survival." (Quoted in Hofstadter, 1955, p. 131)

These ideas—that man is an active constructor of truth, that his ideals and judgments of value are determiners of his activity, and that thought in general is intimately connected with his behavior—are important to the historical transformations of psychology. Undoubtedly the hardheaded, impatient character of the American pioneer directly influenced the shaping of American pragmatism and functionalism, and the contributions of two thinkers, William James and John Dewey, were equally important. Out of an intense dissatisfaction with the psychology they inherited, these men transformed it into something more serviceable. In a real sense, the psychology of beliefs and values was born from this transformation. James considered that the most interesting things about a man are "his ideals and over-beliefs" and that man's "will to believe" is an essential expression of his humanity.

Psychoanalysis

Sigmund Freud can also be viewed as a functionalist. Like James, he found the academic psychology of his day pallid and useless, but as a practicing physician, he had an even greater need for a useful psychology and even less sympathy for nineteenth century structuralism, which he rejected completely.

Freud's concept of wish fulfillment and its relationship to dream symbolism, along with his writings on human motivation, revolutionized psychology and provided a new framework in which to study human values. Freud is as important to the study of values as James was to the study of beliefs. His revolutionary contribution lay in his attempts to show the extent to which certain elemental and universal human needs permeate the whole of human experience, determine man's relation to society, and influence the history and destiny of the human species. From Freud, psychology has learned to respect the power of human values as shapers of experience and action.

Gestalt Psychology and Behaviorism

We read James or Freud today with a great sense of recognition and excitement, for modern psychology has vindicated their criticism of Wundt's structuralism. Indeed, many of their ideas are incorporated directly into contemporary psychological thinking.

But ironically, neither James nor Freud had an immediate revolutionary effect. Despite his brilliant eclecticism, James failed to provide a new and clear vision of what psychology should be and how it should operate. And Freud, in his disdain for experimental procedures, seemed to orthodox psychologists simply to be speaking a different and strange language. While a psychology of beliefs and values could have developed from the thinking of James and Freud, in fact it did not. Two other reformulations of psychology had first to exert their influences.

In the first decade of the twentieth century, a number of controversies engaged the attention of psychologists. One of the most important—the "imageless thought controversy"—was centered in Würzburg, Germany. It concerned the possibility of thinking without images. Is it possible, for example, to think "butterfly" without imagining a butterfly or without imaginging what it would sound like or feel like to say the word? A group of Würzburg psychologists said it was possible, and a group of traditional structuralists (most particularly the American, Titchener) said it was not possible. Both camps produced experiments based on introspective observations, but they could not reach agreement. The attempt to arrive at consensus by means of introspection was a failure. But this very failure provided crucial aid and comfort to those who would venture a new definition of psychology. Two such ventures were particularly important, one German and the other American.

In Germany, The Würzburg controversy and some indigenous philosophic ideas opposed to the elemental British empiricism were important conditions for the formulation of Gestalt psychology, whose fundamental tenets departed radically from those of structuralism (see Koffka, 1935). Gestaltists held that experience has a fundamental unity and wholeness that cannot be analyzed into constituent elements. In the philosophic tradition of Kant, they considered that certain ideas or categories of mind were innate. Experience was still an appropriate object of psychological study, but the Gestalt approach was broadly phenomenological rather than analytically introspective. (A critical difference between phenomenology and introspection is that the former allows the observer to describe experience in natural language while the latter forces him to describe it in the rigidly specified set of terms provided by psychological vocabulary.)

The phenomenalism and the dynamism of Gestalt psychology are extremely important to beliefs and values. Together, these principles encouraged the view that "forces" influence psychological activity and that experience is a product of active commerce with the environment rather than a mere passive registration of what is "out there." The most important link between the Gestalt tradition and a modern psychology of beliefs and values is the work of Kurt Lewin (1936), whose "field theory" will be discussed later in this chapter.

Like Gestalt psychology in Germany, behaviorism developed in the

United States as a reaction to futile issues such as the Würzburg controversy. But the resulting reformulation of psychology was radically different. William James had written earlier that a person's behavior is the key to understanding his thinking. Similarly, William McDougall, in his pioneer social psychology text published in 1908, stated that the primary objective of psychology is to develop an understanding of the causes of behavior.[5] In a sense both James and McDougall were "behaviorists." But the definition of behaviorism that really "took" in American psychology was far more radical than the compromises of James and McDougall.

In 1913, John B. Watson of Johns Hopkins University published what may be considered the manifesto of the behaviorist movement, "Psychology as the Behaviorist Views It." Consciousness, sensations, perceptions, experiences, and all similar mentalistic terms were rejected by Watson as inappropriate objects of psychological study. Watson held that "mind" is a vestige of the theological concept "soul" and has no place in the science of psychology, which is, rather, the science of behavior. We understand an organism's behavior by studying the conditions that cause it to act. Behavior is essentially the organism's response to specific stimulus conditions, and it depends on the nature of the stimulus-response connections that have previously been built into it (learned). Thus, we can understand behavior—all behavior—by knowing what specific stimuli and responses are connected, and how these connections are established.

Like the structuralists, Watson was a thoroughgoing environmentalist. He believed in the almost infinite plasticity of human development. He adopted the principle of reflex conditioning from Pavlov as the paradigm of the learning process, and extended this paradigm by analogy to the most complex forms of acquired skills, including language and thought. He hypothesized that the new organism has a few primary (inherited) action tendencies from which all other "drives" derived. Like the structuralists, Watson used the principles of association in his conceptualization of the learning process.

In one sense, beliefs and values had no place in Watson's behaviorism. Because of their suggestion of mentalism, it was some time before anyone who called himself a behaviorist would use these terms in a psychological discussion. Like structuralism, behaviorism had no place for the problem of knowledge or for a theory of values: habits were substituted for knowledge, and involuntarily acquired goals combined with naturally occurring drives were substituted for values. But behaviorism, like Gestalt psychology, contributed to the development of a psychology of beliefs

---

[5] ". . . psychologists must cease to be content with the sterile and narrow conception of their science as the science of consciousness, and must boldly assert its claim to be the positive science of the mind in all its aspects and modes of functioning, or, as I would prefer to say, the positive science of conduct or behavior" (McDougall, 1908, p. 13).

and values. In this case, the link between the early behaviorist tradition and the contemporary version, which admits beliefs and values, is the work of Edward C. Tolman (1932), who boldly suggested that *purpose* was intelligible from a behaviorist point of view.

With the coming of World War II, many of the important Gestalt psychologists became expatriots in the United States at a time when behaviorism was flourishing. In a latent and inconspicuous way, functionalism survived at the same time as a more or less independent school, especially with the development of the psychology of individual differences, psychological assessment, and industrial, child, and applied psychologies. Pre-war psychology has been described as a set of competing schools (see Heidbreder, 1933). But especially after the war, formerly disparate schools converged in important ways, and these convergences led to an explicit interest in beliefs and values in psychology. Two psychologists, Tolman and Lewin, predominated in the creation of the more pluralistic and theoretically liberal psychology of today.

Lewin's Dynamic Field Theory

Kurt Lewin was educated in Germany in the Gestalt tradition and studied with two founders of that movement, Wertheimer and Koffka. After emigrating to the United States in 1932, he became one of the great innovators in twentieth century psychology.

Frequently, important conceptual advances in a field seem quite simple in retrospect. Perhaps this is a mark of an idea's greatness. In psychology, several of Lewin's conceptions are of this nature. One is the principle of concreteness, which states that only what is concrete has effects. Another is the principle of contemporaneity, or the hypothesis that only present conditions exert an influence on behavior and thinking. Taken together, these two principles comprise Lewin's fundamental orientation to the study of behavior. The person and his psychological environment represent a unified set of concrete circumstances acting at a given point in time. For Lewin, the task of psychology is "to devise ways of treating the full empirical reality of human experience and behavior in a scientific manner without doing violence to them" (quoted in Cartwright, 1959, p. 11).

In considering the determinants of individual thinking and behavior at a given point in time, Lewin developed a special language of psychological description. This language was intended to represent, rather than destroy, an individual's psychological reality; it was drawn from geometry, topological mathematics, and ordinary speech. He spoke of the person acting in a *life space,* which is the totality of psychological influences operating upon a person at a given point in time. The life space is differentiated into regions, corresponding to the individual's conceptual organization of his environment. Regions are charged with valences, which give rise to vectors that attract or repel the person from goal areas. The value of these vectors derives from the attractiveness or desirability of various regions in the life space. The possibility of movement from one region to another is represented by boundaries and barriers in the life space. Lewin introduced the concept *subjective probability* to represent an individual's state of uncertainty about the possibility of achieving a particular objective.

Using these basic conceptions, Lewin was able to represent the dynamics of enormously complex psychological situations—conflicts, frustrations, uncertainties, and so on. He considered the true test of his theory to be its applicability to real-life situations, and thus led psychological research out of the narrow confines of the laboratory.

Lewin's conception of the causal texture of behavior is important for the psychology of beliefs and values. Man's thinking and behaving are inextricably connected for Lewin. Psychological reality for each man is unique; the physical environment influences psychological events only insofar as it is represented in the person's psychological reality. A man's actions depend upon his salient goals as well as upon his conception of the likelihood that these actions will lead to success.

These principles indicate why Lewin is often considered a social psychologist. Man is a social animal, he thinks in social terms, his language is a social instrument, and other people—particularly their affection and disapproval—are among the most influential forces in his life. In sum, Lewin recognized that most of man's decisions are made in relation to a set of social realities.

All the necessary features for a psychology of beliefs and values are present in Lewin's theories. Although he never created a consciously distinct school of psychology, his influence has been enormous. During his lifetime, however, he was a minority voice, for the mainstream of American psychology was neither sympathetic to the somewhat messy nature of the problems that concerned him nor impressed by the logical elegance of his theory. Partly because of the reluctance to accept Lewin's ideas directly, Edward C. Tolman—an avowed behaviorist—becomes important in the development of a psychology of beliefs and values.

Tolman's Purposive Behaviorism

The publication in 1932 of Tolman's *Purposive Behavior in Animals and Men* was an important event in the development of psychology. In this book Tolman argued that it is not a scientific contradiction to speak of organisms as having purposes. In support of this, he invested a great amount of experimental effort in an attempt to understand the behavior of the rat at a choice point in a maze. Tolman hypothesized that the residue of an organism's experience does not merely program the muscles to move in a way that formerly reduced tension but rather enables the organism to anticipate the consequences of his behaviors, and hence to make flexible modifications of them. In his view, organisms develop cognitive maps as a function of experience in their ecology. These maps are composed of expectancies, or means-ends-readinesses, concerning what actions might lead to what consequences in the environment.

Like Lewin, Tolman never constructed a distinct and consistent general psychological theory. But bold theoretical ideas emerged from his acute observations of behavior. Although Tolman was not a mentalist, he was largely responsible for introducing the problem of knowledge to behaviorists. In a late article (Tolman, 1959), he notes that for all practical purposes means-ends-readinesses, expectancies, and beliefs are but different names for the same theoretical construct—a purely cognitive, acquired disposition of the organism. Tolman looked upon cognitive dispositions as "intervening variables"—determinants of behavior that logically fall between existing stimulus conditions (independent variables) and the organism's responses (dependent variables). He was quite careful to avoid the error of considering intervening variables as something real. "My intervening variables are . . . mere temporarily believed-in, inductive, more or less qualitative generalizations which categorize and sum up for me (act as mnemonic symbols for) various empirically found relationships" (Tolman, 1959, p. 97). James would have found it unnecessary to be so cautious, but then James wrote in an era when "mind" was still respectable in psychology.

A number of important ideas influenced Tolman's theories of cognitive psychology. As a graduate student at Harvard, he, along with many others, was swept up by the impressive scientific ambitions and daring new principles of behaviorism. All of his experiments, all of his theoretical ideas, pivot on the observable behavior of organisms. But other influences made him dissatisfied with the "decognified" and overly rigid behaviorism of Watson and his immediate followers. Tolman used both the functionalist ideas of James—the notion that man is an active, striving creature, not a reactive, mechanical robot—and the Gestalt thinking of Lewin, perceiving a certain conceptual geniality between his own behavioral-cognitive theories and Lewin's field theory.

Brunswik and the psychological ecology   Tolman also enjoyed a fruitful and important collaboration with the German psychologist, Egon Brunswik, whom he brought permanently to the University of California in 1937. Brunswik belongs to no distinct school of psychology, for he was an extremely broad and original thinker on the conceptual bases and appropriate methodology of scientific psychology. He argued (1947) that the subject matter of psychology required a distinctive methodology, not a mere copy of the methods employed in the established sciences. Like Lewin, he was impressed with the multiplicity of internal and external factors influencing behavior, and with the necessity of developing a psychology equipped to handle this complexity.

Although wary of the "subjectivism" of Lewin's life space, he was profoundly impressed with the need to develop the concept of a psychological ecology. The term ecology refers to the portion of the environment that supports the life of an organism. By application, the term psychological ecology refers to the aspects of the environment with which the individual interacts and, thus, to the aspects that serve to support and direct his behavior. The way in which psychologists describe the world differs from the descriptions preferred by geologists, meterologists, or zoologists, although there is some overlap with other disciplines. Psychologists include goals, targets, stimulus objects, persons, and groups—to name but a few terms—in their vocabulary for ecological description. The ecological concept will be employed frequently in succeeding chapters of this book.

One aspect of Brunswik's psychological ecology deserves special attention here—namely, its *probabilism*. Brunswik noted that aspects of the physical world are related to each other in a probabilistic fashion. Generally, a person's weight is related to his height, an object's weight is related to its size, a fruit's tenderness is related to its color, and so on. Brunswik considered that an important function of learning is the development of some functional knowledge of these probabilistic physical relationships so that a person might modify his behavior appropriately. For example, he might learn to avoid (by the registration of appropriate cues) attempts to lift very heavy objects. Through an extension of these ideas, Brunswik held that expectancies are probabilistic representations of "what-leads-to-what" in an organism's interactions with its environment.

While Brunswik primarily applied the idea of probabilistic expectancies to perception, Tolman applied it to learning and adaptive behavior. Tolman's outstanding achievement was to give operational, experimental meaning to probabilistic expectancy, and in this manner to establish the behavioral meaning of belief. Values are implied throughout his writings in his conception of a purposive, goal-striving organism. Writing of human behavior, Tolman said that circumstances influence behavior through the mediation of a "belief-value" matrix, by which he seemed to mean those presumed internal dispositions of the person to categorize, interpret, and evaluate the available alternatives for action.

Other Developments Leading to a Psychology of Beliefs and Values

One of the most striking facts about psychology is its tremendous growth and diversification in its short history. Although one hundred years ago there were virtually no psychology departments, psychology courses, or men who identified themselves professionally as psychologists, today more graduate degrees are given in psychology than in all but three other fields—chemistry, engineering, and biology (Office of Education, 1968). The growth of psychology has been especially accentuated since World War II; membership in the American Psychological Association (APA) grew more than 500 percent from 1946 to 1968. Growth in numbers has gone hand-in-hand with professional diversification, so that Divisions (subareas of professional specialty) within the APA numbered 29 in 1968. A great proportion of this growth and diversification is due to the development of applied or "practicing" psychology—industrial, clinical, military, and counseling, for example.

Diversification also brought psychologists into more intimate contact with colleagues in other fields—primarily anthropology, linguistics, biology, physiology, political science, sociology, economics, and applied mathematics, including computer theory and systems analysis. With this contact came an inevitable interchange of concepts and methods, plus the discovery that some problems were remarkably common to several fields.

The term "behavioral science," which has gained currency only in the last decade, is symptomatic of an important redefinition of professional boundary lines. Of particular importance is the development of a "behavioral science" problem area to which none of the traditional disciplines could lay exclusive claim—decision-making. Mathematicians, economists, sociologists, political scientists, and psychologists from a variety of specialized areas have been directly involved with research and theory under this general heading, and the most basic theoretical concepts used have been closely analogous to beliefs and values.

Social psychology   The trend toward diversification has led to the tremendous growth of social psychology since the war. For the most part, pre-war social psychology texts reflect an effort to subsume social behavior under one or another general psychological theory. Thus, McDougall's (1908) book was really a general instinct psychology that extended instincts to complex forms of social behavior. Similarly, F. H. Allport's (1924) text was an attempt to show that social behavior followed the same causal laws of psychology as more simple types of behavior, and that specifically social concepts, such as "group mind" were so much excess theoretical baggage. Similarly, the pre-war book of Miller and Dollard (1941), *Social Learning and Imitation,* was an attempt to extend the principles of classical S-R theory, together with compatible ideas from psychoanalytic theory, to the complex problem of socialization. But after World War II, social psychology began to develop as a distinct division.

The war itself encouraged this development, for public opinions and attitudes were relevant to national conduct during a time of crisis.[6] Hence, methods and concepts were needed that could be directly applied to urgent social problems.

Another important stimulus to the growth of social psychology was provided by the writings of G. H. Mead (1934), who insisted that man is not superficially, but basically, a social animal. A complementary point of view was expressed by Gestalt-oriented Solomon Asch (1952), who argued that social behavior demands its own concepts and methods of study. Asch's seminal text provided several detailed examples of how such an approach to social psychology was experimentally practicable.

End of "grand theories"   The growing liberalism in the character of psychological theory encouraged similar results. Koch (1959) has characterized the period after World War II as a transition from an "Age of Theory" to an epoch in which general theories are taken less seriously and part-theories, or problem-centered theories, are the mode.

One aspect of this shift is the synthesis of new theories from parts of old theories—the new theories being developed for specific applications. In practice, this has meant the development of a number of theories that contain concepts akin to beliefs (expectancies, subjective probabilities, personal constructs) and concepts akin to values (reinforcement value, utility, incentive magnitude, goals, and so on). The diversification in psychology led to the breakdown of "grand theories" and the formulation of theories with a more restricted range of application. Where application has been to social behavior, emerging theories have been quite consistent in their inclusion of cognitive and motivational concepts. Hence, psychology has become more theoretically pluralistic—more eclectic—moving closer and closer to the pragmatic functionalism of James while exhibiting a new sophistication in methodology and experimental technique.

Demands for a psychology of beliefs and values   Each of these developments within psychology and, more broadly, in the behavioral sciences, has been propitious for the furtherance of a more direct concern with beliefs and values. It may be, however, that the most compelling reasons for the development of this kind of study have come from externally imposed demands. For example, in 1950 the classic study on *The Authoritarian Personality* (Adorno, Frenkel-Brunswik, Levinson, and Sanford,

[6] "With World War II, social psychology was 'in demand' by government and military agencies. Studies on propaganda and morale, leadership selection, and 'national character' were needed. Social psychologists were put to work side by side with colleagues who had considered themselves experimental psychologists or sociologists or anthropologists or political scientists" (Sherif, 1963, p. 50).

1950) was published with the specific objective of describing the genesis and operation of anti-Semitic beliefs. This work was parent to a number of other research efforts to understand the psychology of political extremism as well as more general kinds of beliefs (see Rokeach, 1960).

The decades following World War II were filled with a growing recognition of the implications of competing ideological commitments. Since the growth of destructive power has made war an unappealing way to resolve social tensions, interest has perforce been directed to additional strategies for the resolution of political and social conflict. On one level, governments have sponsored large-scale prophetic enterprises, whose business it is to consider possible courses of action in conjunction with the possible responses of an adversary, and on this basis to judge which strategies are most promising for the furtherance of our national interests. The point is that "national interests" are values, and that considering actions and corresponding reactions is, actually, holding beliefs about causal relationships (see Rapaport, 1960).

On another level, the reality of ideological conflicts has made large-scale research projects on how men's minds are changed imperative; a psychology of persuasion, propaganda, brainwashing, conversion, group loyalty, and resistance to stress is demanded by the contemporary conditions of international existence (see Schein, 1956; Lifton, 1956; Frank, 1961).

A growing awareness of the psychological factors that influence scientific thinking has also created a demand for a psychology of beliefs and values. The methods of scientists are but implementations of their beliefs about what techniques are likely to yield satisfactory results. The scientist's choice of problems for study, and the choices made by the scientific community at large, are a reflection of individual and collective value judgments. While psychologists have not always included beliefs and values in their theoretical systems, they have always had beliefs about how psychological inquiry should be conducted and have always made highly operative value judgments concerning the proper objectives of psychology.

Again, a simple observation about the history of science is of great importance—namely, that somebody usually has to support the scientist, because he is generally not directly productive. At least in the United States, psychologists and other scientists are acutely aware of their dependence on other agents of society—usually the government, the trustees of a university, or a granting foundation. The activities of the scientist are in large part determined by the value judgments of these authorities, and by their beliefs about what kinds of research are going to "pay off." Thus, on this level also, there is an obvious need to understand the origins and effects of beliefs and values.

SUMMARY

In this chapter I have presented the paradigm for a psychology of beliefs and values and traced this topic from its origin in philosophy to its treatment in nineteenth and early twentieth century psychology. Finally, I have described the contemporary conditions that show the importance of a psychology of beliefs and values today.

The distinction between believing and valuing was first made by Plato. I have related this distinction to the traditional division within philosophy between the problem of knowledge and the problem of ethics. Although the empiricist position on the problem of knowledge provided the philosophic basis for modern experimental psychology, it also led to the virtual exclusion of that problem from the introspective structural psychology of Wundt and Titchener. The contemporaneous functional psychology of James was very much a "belief-value" psychology, but its influence was less immediate.

In general, the nineteenth century psychological treatment of values was closely related to the post-Darwinian doctrine of instincts in man and the belief that survival was the ultimate value for a species. Beliefs were treated by the early functionalists as a set of psychological realities in terms of which thinking was conducted and from which actions departed.

Psychoanalysis, Gestalt psychology, and American behaviorism, as theoretical rebellions from the narrow futility of introspective structuralism, were important for developing a psychology of beliefs and values. But it was necessary for Lewin to make Gestalt psychology behavioral, for Tolman to make behaviorism cognitive, and for psychoanalytic concepts to become accepted, before a solid conceptual basis was established for theories incorporating both belief and value concepts.

Research on beliefs and values was also influenced by general developments in the behavioral sciences and changes in society itself. The most important influences were (a) the post-war development of social psychology; (b) the fantastic growth and diversification of psychology in general, which gave rise to the formulation of problem-centered, pragmatic theories; (c) the growth of an interdisciplinary approach to problems, one of which is the problem of decision-making; and (d) the contemporary socio-political climate, which demands the development of a psychology of beliefs and values because human conflicts are so frequently framed in these terms.

II

Beliefs

> "When *I* use a word," Humpty Dumpty said, in rather a scornful tone, "it means just what I choose it to mean—neither more nor less."
>
> "The question is," said Alice, "whether you can make words mean so many different things."
>
> "The question is," said Humpty Dumpty, "which is to be master—that's all." **Lewis Carroll**

*T*HIS CHAPTER ATTEMPTS to refine and elaborate the meaning of the term "belief" for the purposes of behavioral analysis. "Belief" has a status similar to such words as "habit" and "percept" in psychological theory. Although each of these terms may be used as a noun, they do not refer to substantive entities but to aspects of psychological functioning— learning, perceiving, or believing. The danger in using these words is that we lapse too easily into thinking of them in substantive terms. Therefore, although it is convenient to continue using the noun "belief," the first refinement of its meaning is to reject its substantive connotations. Beliefs are fictions created to stand for an implicit property of a behaving person. We do not see beliefs like so many eggs or parcels, but rather, we see individuals believ*ing*, know*ing*, or act*ing*.

This "process" orientation toward beliefs has implications for the methods that might be used in their study. One possible mode of studying beliefs might be called phenomenological analysis—an inquiry into how beliefs seem to be experienced. Such analyses have never proceeded very far in the past, and it is doubtful that any attempt here would improve upon James's conclusion: "Belief, the sense of reality, feels like itself—that is about as much as we can say" (James, 1890, Vol. 2, p. 286). And this isn't saying much. If the thinglike character of beliefs is rejected, then it doesn't make sense to worry about what beliefs "really are."

Observations of simple human behaviors provide convincing evidence that individuals are capable of internally representing the external world. Acts—such as depositing a coin in a vending machine, turning a doorknob, buying a postage stamp or a movie ticket, and so on—demonstrate the operation of something like a "cognitive map"[1] about what-leads-to-what—in other words, a set of beliefs.

Two referents for beliefs, or the believing process, have been implied in this discussion. One is the person, including his speech and actions. The other is the external world of facts, events, and relationships. Many of the words in our language imply a duality between beliefs and the objects of beliefs.[2] For example, "true," "rational," "prejudiced," "biased," and "wrong" all imply both beliefs and some standard of comparison for those beliefs—presumably, the facts. Whether or not facts may be found against which to test beliefs is another and troublesome question which we will discuss in Chapter VI. For the present, it is enough to recognize the distinction between an individual's view of reality, which is certainly a matter of belief, and "Reality" itself, which is presumably not dependent upon anyone's belief.[3] Believing is a process that relates

---

[1] See page 16.

[2] The value of psychology's maintaining close relations with ordinary language is well stated by Peters (1958): "The point of looking closely at ordinary usage, if one is a psychologist, is that it often provides a clue to distinctions which it is theoretically important to take account of. We know *so much* about human beings, and our knowledge is incorporated implicitly in our language. Making it explicit would be a more fruitful preliminary to developing a theory than gaping at rats or grey geese" (p. 50).

The reason for scientific resistance to the use of ordinary language is well stated by a philologist, L. P. Smith: "There can be no doubt that science is in many ways the natural enemy of language. Language, either literary or colloquial, demands a rich store of living and vivid words—words that are 'thought-pictures,' and appeal to the senses, and also embody our feelings about emotion or vivid presentation; her [science's] ideal is a kind of algebraic notation, to be used simply as an instrument of analysis; and for this she rightly prefers dry and abstract terms, taken from some dead language, and deprived of all life and personality" (Smith, 1912, pp. 124–125).

There is a third point to be made concerning the choice of vocabulary in psychology. While words from dead languages may be more sterile and less ambiguous for scientific purposes, there is also a danger that scientific coinage may only obscure and make mysterious the meaning of simple metaphors. Sarbin (1967b), for example, makes a strong case that the formidable term "schizophrenia" ("split-mind" in Greek) was an important factor in the unjustified transformation of a descriptive metaphor into a living (if unrecognized) myth; namely, the *disease* of schizophrenia.

Thus, I prefer here to rely upon common-language terms rather than psychological vocabulary. One advantage of discussing beliefs and values in psychology is that there is very little "mystique" to the words themselves.

[3] The avoidance of solipsism here is not based on evidence but upon convenience. The problem of explaining how reality might exist independently of anyone's belief is simply avoided by flat assumption. The following quotation from Russell shows a similar inclination to avoid a solipsism in this manner: "We are thus reduced to the two extreme hypotheses as alone logically defensible. Either, on the one hand, we know principles of nondeductive inference which justify our beliefs, not

the person to the external world. Different beliefs may perform the function of relating well or badly as evidenced by behaviors that might be labeled intelligent or informed, on the one hand, or stupid and naive, on the other.

THE BELIEVING PROCESS

One major difficulty in studying beliefs is the human penchant for dissimulation, for stating one thing while inwardly accepting another. Beliefs may be stated with ease, and on occasion, with very little psychological involvement. It is difficult, therefore, to know what psychological status should be imputed to statements of general belief. It must also be kept in mind that social forces influence the expression of beliefs. The problem that this creates will be discussed in a later section. First, let us consider an example of a belief that quite clearly does not bear this complication.

"A Baltimore woman, who believed her life was doomed by a hex, told her doctors at City Hospital that she would die within three days." This quotation, the report of a phenomenon called "voodoo death," appeared in a Connecticut newspaper. It contains the two major referents for belief previously discussed. The woman is a person in the active process of believing something—her belief is manifest both in her verbal statement and in her coming to the hospital. The external referent for the belief is clearly stated. Either the woman will or will not die within three days—a *fact* is referred to. Thus, the belief may be labled as either true or false. In the example cited, the patient did, in fact, die within three days of the fateful prediction.[4]

The facts to which a belief refers may have occurred in the past, may not yet have transpired, or may belong to both the past and the future, as in the example above. One may believe (with perhaps less

only in other people, but in the whole physical world, including the parts which are never perceived but only inferred from their effects; or, on the other hand, we are confined to what may be called a 'solipsism of the moment,' in which the whole of my knowledge is limited to what I am now noticing, to the exclusion of my past and probably future, also of all those sensations to which, at this instant, I am not paying attention. When this alternative is clearly realized, I do not think that anybody would honestly and sincerely choose the second hypothesis" (Russell, 1948, p. 181.

[4] From the *Meriden Record*, November 18, 1966. According to the article, two of the subject's sisters had perished in a way that exactly coincided with hexes placed upon them. All of the children were born on Friday the 13th, in different years. The immediate cause of death was stated as "primary pulmonary hypertension," which was described as a "fairly rare circulatory problem of the lungs." Physicians agreed that the patient's terror hastened her death.

This case has much in common with reported cases of "voodoo death" among natives of Africa, the West Indies, and certain Pacific islands. W. B. Cannon (1932), was the first to suggest a physiological mechanism for the operation of such curses. He stated that severe psychological tension can interrupt the normal self-regulatory physiological processes of the body—blood pressure, osmotic balance, and so on. Sarbin (1954) has provided an extension of this interpretation in terms of role theory.

than complete certainty) that the New York Yankees won the American League pennant in 1927; or one may believe (again, with some margin of doubt) that the Yankees will win the pennant next year.

It is convenient to refer to the subclass of future-oriented beliefs as *expectancies*. An important psychological problem is to determine the relationship between antecedent events (information) and expectancies about future events. In the example of "voodoo death," the expectancy was acquired from the subject's mother, who was told of the hex by the midwife attending the birth of her children. The strength of the expectancy was greatly augmented by the "successful" operation of the same hex on two elder sisters of the subject.

Some additional examples of expectancies illustrate their common characteristics and point up a number of interesting psychological problems concerning beliefs about future events. Consider the following cases:

1. In Shakspeare's version of the story, Caesar, like the woman from Baltimore, was both forewarned of his impending doom and informed of the date. Yet he appeared not to credit the prophecy and, to his misfortune, disregarded it.

2. If a rat is placed in a T maze, and over a series of trials is rewarded with food more frequently in one arm of the maze than in the other, it develops a behavioral preference for the arm offering the higher probability of food. Within limits, the strength of this preference, measured by the proportion of trials in which the rat chooses one arm over the other, is related to the differences in reward frequencies associated with the two arms of the maze. Thus, it is as if a probablistic expectancy develops concerning the relationship between choice behavior and the administration of food rewards (see Brunswik, 1939; also Tolman & Brunswik, 1935).

3. In 1967, an astrologer in Rio de Janeiro predicted that a "disaster involving thousands of people" would occur at an important soccer game in a nearby state. Even though this story was given large play in headlines the week before the game, attendance was quite unaffected. Happily, the prediction was disconfirmed.

4. It has been repeatedly shown that the behavior of subjects in a psychological experiment is dependent upon expectations—both those of the experimenter and those of the subject—about what is supposed to occur in the experimental setting. Thus, if different groups of experimenters are led to expect different results from some common procedure, data are affected in accord with these expectations (Rosenthal, 1964). If subjects in a hypnosis experiment are carefully given the expectation that some peculiar behavior is characteristic of hypnosis, they tend to act, when they are hypnotized, in a way that is consistent with this (totally manufactured) expectation (Orne, 1959).

Note that in each of these cases there is some informational source for the expectancy—the soothsayer, the direct experience of the rat in the maze, the astrologer, and finally, the experimental psychologist. The form of expectancy transmission varies considerably. Verbal predictions may be direct or vague, and—as in the case of experimental psychologists—the means of communicating expectations may be extremely subtle. For example, subjects may be led to expect a stressful experience by the presence of trays of medical instruments in the experimental setting (Orne & Scheibe, 1964). In the case of the rat in the maze, other non-linguistic cues are used to establish expectations. In a similar manner, a commuter may learn, without being told, that about 60 percent of the time Freeway A is less congested than Freeway B and thus may develop a preference for the former.

Another way to compare these examples of expectancies is by their outcomes. In each of the first three cases an outcome occurred that either confirmed or disconfirmed the expectation—Caesar was killed, the rats were fed, and soccer fans were not harmed. In the fourth case there was also an outcome, but of a different kind. In this case, the outcome was directly dependent upon the expectation itself. It is as if the prediction was the determinant of its own outcome.

Robert K. Merton (1948) called the phenomenon represented by the fourth example the "self-fulfilling prophecy." A dramatic example is provided in some recent research on the determinants of achievement in primary school children. The hypothesis was that teachers form expectations of children's ability levels before they have an adequate basis for making such judgments, and that they communicate these expectations to the children in a way that actually influences their achievement. In a study by Rosenthal and Jacobson (1968), teachers were given completely arbitrary predictions that some pupils had high achievement potential. These predictions were reflected in an actual acceleration of performance for those pupils. Beliefs about future occurrences are often important determinants of those occurrences, for they influence the choices that are made, the chances that are taken, and the hypotheses that are adopted as working assumptions.

The Probabilistic Character of Beliefs

Aristotle stated that there are four degrees of assurance about a proposition. The highest degree is complete *certainty,* next is *belief,* then *suspicion,* and finally *doubt* (Lewinsohn, 1961). Although the categorical treatment of assurance levels is not to be preserved here, the distinctions offered by Aristotle are supported by the previously given examples of the operation of expectancies. It is reasonable to suppose that Caesar placed less credence in the warning of the soothsayer than the woman from Baltimore did in the warning of the midwife, for the latter seemed to accept her doom as a certainty. To draw from another example, it is clear that the odds assigned to a horse before a race represent degrees of belief in the possibility that the horse will win the race. Similarly, weather predictions are currently made in the form of probability statements, such as, "The probability (or chance) of precipitation tomorrow is 70 percent."

Degree of belief is important because it determines dispositions to act on certain assumptions. A person's willingness to pursue a course of action depends to a great extent upon his confidence of success. A boat of doubtful or suspicious seaworthiness attracts fewer passengers than a vessel considered with virtual certainty to be sound.

The problem of different degrees of certainty or "partial belief" is one that demands some appropriate means of reference or representation. There seems no good reason for drawing strict distinctions between "belief" and "certainty," for example. Some people seem certain of their assertions and others seem to doubt them even while accepting them. Both Lewin and Brunswik were acutely aware of the problem of psychological uncertainty, and each suggested that Aristotle's categorical distinctions be eliminated in favor of a continuous dimension. This suggestion was implemented by considering degrees of certainty to be representable by, or analogous to, mathematical probabilities.

Probabilities may range from zero to one. If the probability used to describe an event is either zero or one, the possibility of variability is denied—either the event will occur or it will not. Probabilities between zero and one token some degree of variation, some margin of doubt, however small, that the event will or will not occur. Indeed, the magnitude of a probability is meant to refer, even in mathematical theory, to the likelihood that some specific event will occur under certain specified conditions. Flipping an ordinary coin many times will yield about one-half heads and one-half tails, and the probability associated with each of these outcomes is considered to be one-half.

There is a good argument that the basis of all probability statements is subjective or psychological. That is, probabilities derive from a degree of belief that some specific thing will happen (see Savage, 1954). In any case, it seems natural to let probabilities qualify beliefs on a psychological dimension. The position taken here is that the believing process is played out between the limits of zero and one—that every belief could conceivably be tagged with a number in this range (including the limiting points) to represent the mixture of certainty and doubt on any proposition.

By way of summary, beliefs have information sources, although the character of these sources may vary widely. Expectations, an important subclass of beliefs, refer to the future and guide overt behavior. Crude categorizations of degree of belief (certainty, belief, suspicion, and doubt) do not seem representative of how people actually think. The mathematical concept of probability, which is strongly related in any case to psychological judgments, is a fitting solution to the problem of qualifying degree of belief. Thus, beliefs are considered to vary quantitatively (between, and including, zero and one) according to degree of certainty. The higher the certainty, the higher the probability associated with the belief. For example, a person may be very certain when he begins to cross a footbridge that the bridge will not collapse. The probability associated with this belief would be nearly one. On the other extreme, a person walking in the rain may consider it highly unlikely that lightning would strike him. The probability associated with this belief would be near zero.

The Interaction of Proximal and Distal Uncertainties

There are two distinct sources of uncertainty about the occurrence of events. One arises because of the unreliability of relationships in the ecology. Thus, one cannot be perfectly certain that a balloon will not burst when inflated because of possible undetected defects in the balloon. This is *distal* uncertainty. Part of the uncertainty about the balloon, however, may also be due to the imperfect skill or technique of the inflater. This is *proximal* uncertainty.

Quite obviously, the relative contributions of proximal and distal uncertainties differ for each event. Virtually all the uncertainty about winning a lottery is distal. By contrast, expectations of being able to find rhymes (without a book) are based upon proximal uncertainty. However, in most situations of behavioral choice, both proximal factors (skill) and distal factors (chance) influence the formation of expectancies.

Cohen and his collaborators devised a series of experiments to study how these two components of uncertainty combine in the production of a single expectancy of success at some task (Cohen, Dearnaley, & Hansel, 1958a, 1958b). The experimental procedure used variations on a simple dart game; size of target, composition of target, throwing distance, and the sharpness of the dart were manipulated to produce varying combinations of skill and chance factors in the game. For example, a subject may have been asked how many times out of five he expected to place a dart in a target of a certain size and at a certain distance, if on each trial he were assured a sharp dart but had to take a one-in-five chance of drawing a metal rather than a cork target. Although the results are tentative, they indicate that proximal and distal sources of uncertainty are operationally distinct and that the origin of uncertainty determines the kind of "mental arithmetic" used in making expectancy statements.

Recent research on a personality variable known as Internal-External Control (see Rotter, 1966) has provided further evidence of this distinctiveness. The variable is designated as a measure of an individual's tendency to view personally relevant events as internally (proximally) or externally (distally) caused. Some individuals consider their own skills and capacities the major determinants of any successes or failures. Others generally feel that they are victims or beneficiaries of chance factors. According to self-report data, the internal disposition is characteristic of more effective, achievement-oriented personalities, and the external is characteristic of more submissive and socially maladjusted individuals (Hersch & Scheibe, 1967).

Thus, both in personality research and in laboratory studies of simple games, proximal and distal sources of uncertainties have been distinguished as sources of behavioral expectancies. This distinction will be important to a number of applications presented in Chapters V and VI.

Risk and Uncertainty

Acting on the basis of a probabilistic expectancy involves taking a risk. But there is a distinction between *known* risks (for example, the risk of losing on a single play of a roulette wheel) and *unknown* risks (for example, the risk that an untried drug will have harmful effects). Conventionally, decisions made when the probabilities associated with outcomes are well known are described as *risky decisions,* while decisions made when the probabilities are not well known are described as *uncertain* (Luce & Raiffa, 1957). Thus, a single probability index may not sufficiently describe the psychological situation of uncertainty. Another probability number may be required to stand for the extent to which a person has *confidence* in belief-probabilities.[5] Confidence in the probabilities of risky decisions is high, and for uncertain decisions it is low.

The psychological significance of this distinction is well illustrated in an anecdote reported by C. A. Mace in his Foreword to Cohen's (1960) *Chance, Skill and Luck:*

> Shortly before the General Election of 1959 a businessman dining at Oxbridge College found himself seated next to a very distinguished statistician and psychologist. The conversation very understandably turned to the grounds for the then prevailing opinion that it was going to be a very near thing: either party might get in by a very small majority. But the statistician said: "I have looked at all the evidence, but whichever way I look at it the evidence points to a clear and substantial majority for the Conservative Party."
>
> A few days after the election the businessman met the statistician again, and thanked him warmly for what he had taken as advice. "Yes," he said, "I bought Steels and made a very handsome capital profit. I hope you did as well."
>
> "No," said the statistician sadly, "I had not the courage of my convictions."

[5] Students familiar with statistics will recognize that the distinction between a probability associated with a belief and the confidence in that probability is strictly analogous to the distinction between the Expected Value and the Standard Error of a sampling distribution.

In terms of the present discussion, the businessman had great confidence in the high probability of a Conservative victory, while the statistician, similarly judging that probability to be high, was not confident that his judgment was correct.

BELIEFS AND PSYCHOLOGICAL REALITY

The preceding paradigm for beliefs suggests that their function is behavioral guidance. Tolman's concept of a cognitive map is but a metaphorical extension of this idea. A map is a representation of reality, but as a representation it is approximate, highly schematic, and extremely partial to some features of reality as opposed to others. Just as there are innumerable ways of mapping the same territory—topography, transportation routes, weather conditions, population density, type of vegetation, varieties of fish and wildlife, geologic features, and so on—so there are innumerable ways of developing a psychological schematization of reality. But note that each way of preparing a geographic map is done with a specific purpose in view. Similarly, psychological representations of reality are functional—they are prepared with a purpose.

The idea that our views of psychological reality are functional is hardly new, and like many ideas, once stated it seems obvious. Initially, however, there may be some resistance to this view of things, for it seems to imply that our stable, reliable, and rational reality should be replaced by a perfectly arbitrary chaos. This is not really a proper implication, however, for the schematic, partial, and approximate character of representations of reality does not necessarily indicate either arbitrariness or chaos. The idea that must be sacrified is that any man can be a perfectly impartial observer of the reality that confronts him. As Royce (1894) noted, the "great question for every truth-seeker is: In what sense, to what degree, with what motive, for what end, may I and should I be prejudiced?" (p. 323). That is, What kind of partial map of reality should be drawn?

A variety of names have been proposed at different times to stand for the congeries of beliefs that comprise a person's world view. The Lewinian conception of the life space has already been noted. In addition, Cantril has proposed the terms "assumptive world" (Cantril, 1950) and "psychological reality" (Cantril, 1965). In keeping with Brunswik's probabilistic functionalism, the term "modular organization" has been suggested as an implicit functional representation of ecological relationships (Sarbin, Taft, & Bailey, 1960). Kelly (1955) has employed the phrase "personal construct system" in a similar sense. In each of these cases the central idea is that there is nothing *absolute* about man's conception of reality, and that his thinking and consequent behavior are strongly conditional upon his particular and partial way of construing things.

Man's collective conception of himself and his relation to the world is undergoing radical revision. Men formerly thought that the earth was flat and at the center of the universe, that man was a special divine creation, that there were only four basic elements, that madness was caused by the moon, that atoms were irreducible particles, that the heart was the seat of the soul, and so on. Copernicus, Darwin, Galileo, along with modern surgeons and many others, have done a great deal to modify these ideas, but no fixed picture of how things *really* are has emerged. Rather the progress of science, or more generally, of learning, is a mechanism forcing the continual reorganization of beliefs. In this process, of course, man's symbolic and linguistic skills have played a large part.[6]

But while the psychological universe of an individual and of the human species as a whole may undergo continual revision and development, a person's way of thinking and acting at any instant is a function of the particular construction of reality that happens to be "in place"; he thinks in the terms and with the categorical distinctions that are available to him at that point. Thus, the same events may be referred to different classes, depending upon the distinctions a person is accustomed to making.

For example, bizarre and deviant behavior has been looked upon at different times in the following ways:

a. as the result of *demons* entering a person and exerting their forces to deform him

b. as an imbalance in the *four natural humours* of the body (blood, black bile, yellow bile, and phlegm)

c. as *moral weakness,* or weakness of *personal will*

d. as the product of a *diseased mind,* and hence a legitimate concern of medical practitioners

e. as due to an unfortunate history of *conditioning* for the circumstances in which a person must live

f. as the result of *conflicting* or *inappropriate social conventions*

g. as *unrecognized unconscious impulses* creating sufficient *intrapsychic tension* to incapacitate the person for social behavior[7]

---

[6] "It is symbolic thought which overcomes the natural inertia of man and endows him with a new ability, the ability constantly to reshape his human universe" (Cassirer, 1954, p. 86).

[7] The invention and organization of concepts to explain deviant behavior is probably a functional necessity. Problems arise however when the categories created survive into epochs when ways of thinking are different. The following quotation, from a very enlightening book on this question, illustrates one such shift in thinking: "To put it simply and bluntly, nothing can be said, by the canons of modern philosophy of science, of the existence of the unconscious as a substantive entity; the assertion of its existence is in principle untestable and hence meaningless. To ask whether the unconscious exists is analogous to asking whether the soul or God exists: One either acts on the assumption that they do or do not. If we consider it as a theoretical construct, we simply doubt the utility or the necessity of its existence. The unconscious represents the outcome of interpretative analysis, and an ill-conceived one at that" (Levy, 1963, p. 22).

The italicized words in these phrases represent the distinctive psychological realities of a variety of psychological authorities. If an authority from each category were seated in the same room, and a subject entered and fell to gnawing the carpet, each authority would probably think he had seen a manifestation of his own theory. The differences in what was seen, of course, can be traced to preexisting differences among those who did the seeing. "The empiricist," said Santayana, "thinks he believes only what he sees—but he is much better at believing than at seeing."

A well-debated principle of linguistics is closely related to this point. The principle is that the language of a culture defines the limitations and possibilities of thinking within that culture—that a distinctive world view is associated with each language. This idea is referred to as the Whorf-Sapir hypothesis, or the "principle of linguistic relativity" (see Whorf, 1956; Greenberg, 1966). On a technical level there is good reason to doubt that this principle is generally true, for it implies certain theoretical limits on the translation of thought from one language to another that have not been empirically demonstrated, and it also implies a much higher relationship between verbal fluency and intelligence than has been found (see Lenneberg, 1964).

It may be that two persons are capable of evolving a psychological reality (or cognitive structure) sufficient for the translation and mutual understanding of ideas. However, it is perfectly obvious that unless the psychological realities of the two persons are made to overlap, their thinking will differ in process and content. Let an uninitiated person try to solve a problem in topological mathematics, for example; or let the student ignorant of astrophysics try to solve a problem having to do with the "red shift"; or let the physicist try to follow the jargon of teenagers; or let the mathematician try to understand a group of social scientists discussing "social structure and dynamics." It is obvious that communication demands a shared language. However, everyone who speaks English does not speak the *same* English, and the division of languages into English, French, Portuguese, Chinese, and so on, is partially arbitrary. Further, there are a host of sublanguages. Ultimately, each individual has an idiosyncratic language that defines, with its communalities with other languages, the ability of the person to communicate with, think like, and understand other people.

Words, Categories, Beliefs, and Expectancies

One of the most important functions of words is to serve as labels for categories. Thus, "cow" is a label for a class of environmental objects. According to Bruner (1957), a "category may be regarded as a set of specifications regarding what events will be grouped as equivalent—rules respecting the nature of critical cues required" (p. 232) for acceptance or rejection of an event as an instance of a category. Thus, a particular set of cues—four legs and a tail, a certain sound, and certain structural characteristics—comprise the definition of the "cow" category. Functionally, the presence of the cues is critical to acceptance of an object as equivalent to other members of the group (in this instance, the group "cow").

Beliefs may refer to the existence of categories, or to the possibility that events exist that satisfy the requirements of a particular category. A unicorn may be defined as a "horselike beast with a single horn emerging from the middle of its forehead." Given this definition of the category, the question arises as to whether there are any actual instances of unicorns. To say, "I don't believe in unicorns," is not to deny the rules for defining the category, but rather, to say that when these rules are applied, it is doubtful that living examples of the class can be found. It is still possible, even without believing in them, to talk about unicorns—the mythology surrounding them, their supposed properties, and perhaps their function within a particular folk mentality.[8]

The ability to talk about categories that do not coincide with any environmental examples is not a trivial characteristic of human thinking. Much scientific discussion is carried on in these terms. In this sense, unicorns are fully as legitimate as electron shells, pi-mesons, engrams, n-dimensional hyperspaces, antimatter, or genes—all are functional constructions, made up to help men understand one or another kind of problem.

Beliefs may also refer to conceived relationships among cognitive categories. Thus, "cows eat grass" is a statement of relational belief, as is "lead is heavier than aluminum" or "Shakespeare lived after Dante." These statements also imply some understanding of the relational operators "eat," "heavier than," and "lived after," and this understanding in turn implies the acceptance of still other belief categories—food, weight, and time. Moreover, it is likely that a great number of implicit relational beliefs can be made explicit on demand—by inferential extension and combination with other beliefs. Thus, a person would probably agree that neither Shakespeare nor Dante was ever in danger of being eaten by cows, that a life-size aluminum statue of either man would be lighter than a copy made of lead, that grass existed both before and after Dante, and so on.

The distinction between categories that have environmental referents (for instance, cows) and those that do not (for instance, unicorns) is not of critical importance to most psychological functions. For many relational beliefs, most or all of the terms are fictitious. For example, "Huckleberry Finn went down the Mississippi on a raft with Negro Jim," "The

---

[8] See Shepard (1930) for a very interesting exercise of this kind on precisely the topic of unicorns.

mean of a positively skewed frequency distribution is always to the right of the mode," "Zeus was the son of Chronus," or "A disjunction between social norms and legitimate opportunities produces anomie." If these examples were used on true-false examinations in classes of, respectively, American literature, descriptive statistics, Greek mythology, and urban sociology, they would be accepted as serious and sensible. Other relational beliefs combine the fictitious and the real types of category. For example, "Susan Brown is suffering from anomie," or "That child is more rebellious than Huckleberry Finn."

Relational beliefs that involve the self as one of the categories have special psychological significance. By means of such beliefs, a person defines himself, compares himself with others, and forms expectations about future successes and failures. In Chapter VI we will see some implications of the view that social identity is comprised of a set of beliefs about the self.

The Thicket in the Quagmire—And a Way Out

At this point it may seem that things are rather complicated. If by "psychological reality" we mean the sum total of beliefs—existential and relational, abstract and concrete, expectational and historical, self-oriented and other-oriented, and if it is operationally possible to combine these characteristics of beliefs, and if each belief must be qualified by both a probability and a region of confidence about that probability, then we can see that "psychological reality" is as complicated and impenetrable as a construct can be. A wiring diagram for the human mind would take a lot of paper.

But then it should.

Fortunately, much of the complexity disappears when we realize that the picture of "psychological reality" presented here is partially misleading in that it suggests a massive, interlaced structure that just sits there. The functional view of things is different and more reassuring.[9]

---

[9] James expresses this difference very well: "My thinking is first and last and always for the sake of my doing, and I can only do one thing at a time. A God,' which is supposed to drive the whole universe abreast, may also be supposed, without detriment to his activity, to see all parts of it at once and without emphasis. But were our human attention so to disperse itself we should simply stare vacantly at things at large and forfeit our opportunity of doing any particular act. A Mr. Warner, in his Adirondack story, shot a bear by aiming not at his eye or heart, but 'at him generally.' But we cannot aim 'generally' at the universe; or if we do, we miss our game. Our scope is narrow, and we must attach things piecemeal, ignoring the solid fulness in which the elements of Nature exist, and stringing one after another of them together in a serial way, to suit our little interests as they change from hour to hour. In this, the partiality of one moment is partly atoned for by the different sort of partiality of the next. To me now, writing these words, emphasis and selection seem to be the essence of the human mind. In other chapters other qualities have seemed, and will seem, more important parts of psychology" (1890, Vol. 2, pp. 333–334).

Functionally, beliefs appear in the context of behavior. Thus, it doesn't make much sense to ask how many beliefs a person has, or the precise way in which a complete set of beliefs is defined. As a point of departure, the concept of an enormously complex cognitive structure is helpful, for it suggests the enormous range of functional capacities that man is known to have. But we must remember that this is only an *implicit* structure; actual beliefs arise from the interaction between this implicit structure and specific situational demands. Thus beliefs are, in a sense, peculiar to the particular situation.

The methodological implication is that an expressed belief is never free of situational constraints. When the priest asks specific questions in a catechism, appropriate belief responses emerge with dependable regularity and uniformity. The same questions put to the same persons, but at a different time and place, might call forth somewhat more idiosyncratic and qualified beliefs. To be sure, it is possible to generalize about a person's beliefs—to assert that he will act on occasion B in a way that is consistent with his actions on occasion A. But this is always an empirical matter—protracted consistency of expressed beliefs may or may not be observed. The world has too much heresy and hypocrisy—or to use words with a different color, courage and originality—not to note the fact.

Apparent inconsistencies in manifestations of belief are reconciled when we acknowledge the extent to which situation and belief are tied to each other. Campbell (1963) notes that some whites who say they regard blacks as equals occasionally act as if they regarded them as inferiors. This kind of inconsistency on a national level inspired Myrdal (1944) to write of the "American dilemma"—the coexistence of the verbal principle of human equality with the obvious fact of discrimination. Functionally, this is really no dilemma, for it is meaningless to ask what a person's *real* beliefs (independent of time and circumstance) are about blacks. Beliefs are not "thinglike," as noted at the beginning of this chapter. The principle of human equality and the practice of human discrimination function at different levels, and when the difference in levels is understood, the difference in apparent belief is also.

Most human societies hold persons accountable for statements and deeds performed under diverse circumstances and at different times. The norm of personal consistency is socially imposed. Thus, children are told that it is wrong to lie, to attack or be angry with people they are supposed to love, or to conduct themselves in an undignified manner in a holy place. But the enforcement of the norm of consistency is selective, and many "contradictions" are allowed exemption from this principle. The existence of extensive crime by "noncriminals" (white-collar crime), the relation of religious creed to daily life, the mixture of contradictory religious systems (spiritualism and Catholicism in Brazil, for example; see Pierson, 1967)—these are but some of the more common examples of tolerated inconsistencies. The behavior of subjects on psychological tests shows the same kind of contradiction. Kroger (1967) has shown that subjects who took an interest test under military conditions showed a more military "profile" than a carefully matched group of subjects who took the same test under different circumstances. This implies that one individual might assent to contradictory assertions about himself, depending upon the circumstances. Unfortunately, there is no experimental evidence on this possibility. Herman Melville is said to have remarked that the only truly consistent characters are the contrived inventions of novelists and biographers.

Thus, in order to understand how beliefs operate in the production of psychological conflict it is necessary to study them both within the particular situation and within the broad cultural context. This is but an extension of the simplifying principle stated at the beginning of this section—that beliefs are emergent guides for purposive behavior in specific situations.

Assessment and Veridicality[10]

It is now possible to consider the closely related problems of assessment and evaluation of beliefs. The problem of assessment is that of describing a person's operative views of how the world is put together, of what goes with what, of what causes what. The problem of evaluation is that of comparing the results of such an assessment with some external standard or criterion. The difficulties in assessing and evaluating beliefs stem from a common source: the equivocal relationship between beliefs and the external world of facts they are supposed to represent. Beliefs go considerably beyond the raw sense information that is supplied by the physical world, and assessment of them is strongly affected by the choice of method and situation of measurement, as noted in the preceding section.

Sarbin, Taft, and Bailey (1960) note the following sources for beliefs:

1. Induction: the development of a generalized belief based on a summation of past observations. For example, through repeated confirmatory experiences, a person might build up the expectation that "red apples are good to eat."

2. Construction: the adoption of a theory about relationships (be-

---

[10] The term "veridicality" is taken from the psychology of perception and refers to the coincidence of a perceptual report (assessment) with actual characteristics of some target. For example, a subject may respond to a color blindness test by correctly or incorrectly reporting the configurations presented. If he responds correctly, his perception is said to be veridical.

lief), which may or may not be based on inductive reasoning. "Some aspects of [the] theory . . . may be created out of fantasy products. . . . [For instance] The presence of sunspots may be associated with the potential for homicide" (Sarbin *et al.,* 1960, p. 49).

3. Analogy: the formation of a belief based on observed similarities among things or events. If A is like B in some respects, the analogy is often drawn that A is like B in other—unobserved—respects. For example, a person might observe that both oranges and tangerines are approximately spherical, orange fruits having a firm skin. He might then form the belief that oranges and tangerines have a similar taste.

4. Authority: the maintenance of a belief based upon information received on the authority of others. Obviously, a large number of beliefs are acquired in this way. Probably the majority of people who believe the earth is round, that Napoleon once lived, that the world is in danger of a population explosion, and that Russia has a 100-megaton bomb base their beliefs on someone else's authority.

There is good experimental evidence that expectancies are formed inductively from continual commerce with the ecology. For example, Attneave (1953) demonstrated a very strong relationship between the actual frequency with which letters are used in English and judgments of those frequencies. Underwood (1966) has reviewed a number of similar studies with words and other common stimulus materials and concluded that many environmental probabilities are well represented in persons' judgments.

All of this is consistent with the view of mental development implied by Locke's epistemology—event probabilities are gradually assimilated from the ecology. A good deal is known about the information-processing characteristics of the human being with respect to input (see Miller, 1956), but unfortunately this leaves us a long way from understanding the complete nature of belief systems in intelligent adults. In psychophysics the veridicality problem is to ascertain the relationship between physical measurements and psychological effects, such as judging the heaviness of objects. For simple expectancies (as in Attneave's study with English letters), the problem is methodologically as well as theoretically the same. However, we must consider other and more complex kinds of beliefs.

Galanter (1962) has demonstrated that it is possible to get reliable belief statements in the form of probabilities concerning various contemplated events. For example, he found that the psychological probability of surviving an airplane crash was somewhat less than the probability that the National League would win the next World Series and somewhat greater than the judged likelihood that someone could bicycle nonstop from Philadelphia to New York. The point of obtaining information on such arcane possibilities was to demonstrate that "techniques of direct estimation of magnitudes of events for which there are no obvious underlying physical continua is a perfectly feasible procedure" (p. 216). It is methodologically sensible to look upon beliefs as probabilistic, even though it is not possible to compute the actual probabilities of the ecological events to which the beliefs refer.

The confidence with which beliefs are stated has also been subject to investigation. Adams and Adams (1961) assembled and administered a questionnaire of true and false items based on a world almanac. At the same time, they obtained ratings of the confidence with which true-false answers were given. They found a strong relationship between the rated degree of confidence in a response and the likelihood that the response was correct. This relationship deteriorated for individuals whose thinking was considered erratic and inefficient—that is, a group of hospitalized schizophrenics. "Confidence" is used here, as earlier in the chapter, to signify the margin of doubt about the correctness of a statement of belief.

Thus, it is possible to develop reliable and meaningful assessments of two distinct kinds of beliefs—those for which objective criteria of correctness exist, and those for which no such criteria exist. The subject in a probability learning experiment, for example, estimates event occurrences with a relative frequency that is then compared directly to the actual frequency of those occurrences. In this case, objective criteria are obtainable. But it is also meaningful to quantify beliefs about such possibilities as the existence of ESP, the long term effects of nuclear fallout, or the course that race relations will take in the United States. Fishbein and Raven (1962) have obtained data on just these questions, using an adaptation of Osgood's (Osgood, Suci, & Tannenbaum, 1957) semantic differential technique.[11] They found quite reliable ratings of these questions on scales of probable-improbable, possible-impossible, likely-unlikely, existent-nonexistent, and true-false.

The difficulty is that the relationship has seldom been demonstrated between beliefs assessed in this manner and actual decisions and actions outside the setting of psychological experiments. It is one thing to assess a belief reliably, for this demands only a consistency of response under carefully controlled circumstances, but quite another to verify the validity of these beliefs as predictors of behavior in other settings.

Perhaps this problem will be clarified by an example. A creed may be repeated precisely and reliably under similar circumstances over a period of years. Yet in open forum, in a psychiatrist's office, in a business office, or at a convention, the beliefs entailed in this creed may be expressly

---

[11] The semantic differential is a technique devised by Osgood in which the subject rates topics on a series of single-dimension scales. For example, a subject might be asked to rate himself and then his father on a series of five-point scales labeled "good-bad," "aggressive-passive," "calm-anxious," "weak-strong," and so on.

negated. The extent to which measured beliefs are generalized over situations and methods of assessment is a matter to be determined by observation.[12]

A basic problem for the assessment of beliefs—whether or not external referents or stimulus dimensions are obtainable—is that the behavior used as an index of belief is necessarily influenced by values as well. Siegel (1964) provided a direct example of this in a series of experiments on decision making. Using a simple two-light stimulus display, he obtained the customary matching of frequency of guesses for each light and actual frequency of occurrence of that light over a series of trials. Thus, if the right light appeared on 75 percent of the trials, the proportion of "right light" predictions came to approach 75 percent. However, when he introduced special rewards for maximizing the number of correct choices, predictions were deflected accordingly, so that the 75 percent light came to be predicted almost 100 percent of the time.

The conformity experiments by Asch (1952) demonstrate a similar principle. Under normal circumstances, a person may state his judgments and beliefs in a relatively unconstrained manner. But the presence of a group of people who consistently disagree with him is usually sufficient to alter what he says he thinks, sees, or believes (see Crutchfield, 1955). Again, there is no way of describing what a person "really" believes, for expressions of belief are always gathered under circumstances that may deflect or distort.

SUMMARY

Functionally, beliefs are guides to action. Through commerce with the ecology, an individual develops a set of functional dispositions, or a "belief system," which are implicit expectations concerning what leads to what. However, because relationships in the real world are often imperfect and because experience with this world is partial and incomplete, beliefs must be qualified as probabilistic. Predictive beliefs (expectancies) may be stated in probabilistic terms; for example, the chance of rain is 70 percent. *Confidence* refers to the strength of the belief and implies a margin or range of probabilities.

Two components of uncertainty contribute to the formation of expectancies. Most personally relevant events are partially determined by proximal (internal) factors, such as skill and capacities, and partially by distal (external) factors, such as slight variations in features of the environment.

[12] "The inconsistency of acting on two opposite principles, however it may vex the soul of the philosopher, rarely troubles the common man; indeed he is seldom even aware of it. His affair is to act, not to analyze the motives of his action. If mankind had always been logical and wise, history would not be a long chronicle of folly and crime" (Frazer, 1961, p. 163).

Proximal and distal factors included, belief systems form a peculiar construction of psychological reality, which goes far beyond "the data given," and which serves as a basis for the categorization, recognition, and organization of new experiences. Therefore, thinking and communication are contingent upon the nature of this psychological reality. Functionally, categorical distinctions and relational beliefs do not need referents in the distal ecology in order to serve important psychological purposes. Scientific theories and primitive mythologies are but two obvious examples of such functional fictions.

Beliefs are serially evoked by changing exigencies throughout a segment of time. Thus, the expression of a belief is a highly contingent matter. Consistency in that expression may not be inherent but externally imposed and enforced by social norms. Even the enforcement of that norm is often itself inconsistent and discriminatory.

The accuracy (veridicality) of many kinds of beliefs about the external world can be tested. Judgments about the relative frequency of various events may be compared with an independent count of those events. A number of studies show that accurate probabilistic expectancies are formed for certain classes of events.

But for many other beliefs no external referent is evident, and here the question of veridicality is not meaningful except in an indirect sense. A theory or a religion may be considered good or correct if it works—that is, if it produces results or makes people happy. This is a criterion of sorts, even though direct tests of the propositions involved in the religion or the theory are not feasible.

It appears that the expression of a belief is influenced by *values* as well as by the disposition to give credence to a proposition. Therefore, we will now direct our attention to the topic of values.

III

Values

De gustibus non est disputandum.

PROCLAIMING that tastes are not arguable is usually a way of terminating rather than beginning a discussion. Whatever the merit of the idea that "there is no accounting for tastes," evidence abounds that psychologists have not taken it seriously, for many a career has been devoted to just such an accounting. Out of this concern has grown the complex and self-contradictory subject known as the psychology of motivation. The purpose of this chapter is to abstract some order from the confusion surrounding motivation so that we can delimit the term "value."

THE VALUING PROCESS

Distinguishing Between Beliefs and Values

One fundamental distinction between beliefs and values derives from the philosophical differentiation between questions of fact and questions of value. There is a difference between asking, "What is true (or likely)?" and, "What is good (or preferable)?" Examples of the former type of question are, "Which is the shortest route between Albany and Pittsburgh?" and, "Do you have any strawberries for sale?" Examples of the latter are, "Which is the best route from Albany to Pittsburgh?" and "Are those strawberries good?" As was noted in the previous chapter, answers to questions of fact are belief statements. Answers to questions of value, then, are value judgments. Belief statements refer to what is possible, what exists, what happened in history, what a person is, what he can do. They are framed in terms of expectancies, hypotheses, subjective probabilities, assumptive worlds, cognitive maps, and so on. Value judgments

41

refer to what is wanted, what is best, what is desirable or preferable, what ought to be done. They suggest the operation of wishes, desires, goals, passions, valences, or morals.

Value Standards

An important distinction between beliefs and values concerns standards of veridicality. For beliefs, we are often able to use external criteria of reality. In this manner, many beliefs can be labeled "true or false." But while people in disputes may call their opponents' values false, the standards by which they arrive at such a judgment are not so obvious. Clearly, arguments may concern differences in values as well as differences in beliefs. The phrase, "You don't know what's good"—probably used most frequently by parents to their offspring—is an example of a value disputation.

Standards of value are central to normative ethics in philosophy, yet few normative principles find broad or universal agreement. *Facts,* on the other hand, are a matter of descriptive science, in which there is more—if not complete—agreement. Galileo's main appeal to those with primitive beliefs was simply to observe the evidence. In normative ethics, no similar admonition commands assent. Instead, there is the paradox and contradiction of competing ethical systems. Christ brought an ethical revolution, reversing the conventionally construed worldly good. Neitzsche considered the Christian ethic degrading and destructive, and thus was able to proclaim himself at once the most wicked and yet most beneficent man who ever lived. Some modern existentialists reject all general approaches and instead concentrate on a "morality of the moment," wherein rightness resides in the uniqueness of circumstance. From these few examples we can see that it is harder to argue values than to argue facts.

But values may be evaluated in a limited way. If a given system of values is accepted by a group of people, it makes sense to talk about values as "right and wrong" within that context. For instance, in an economic context, a "good sense of values" might refer to the ability to make accurate estimates of prices within an economic system. Many individuals who seem not to share the dominant values of society—for instance, criminals, dope addicts, prostitutes, and mental patients—are either punished or treated for their deviance. Thus, while the problem of value standards is difficult to solve, the philosophical problem of normative ethics clearly has a psychological counterpart—the problem of socialization, or the acquisition by individuals of the values held in their social environment.

To grasp the psychological problems of socialization and deviance, we must have some understanding of how personal values are described. This is analogous to descriptive ethics in philosophy. The question is, "What *is* valued?" rather than, "What *should be* valued?"

Values and Preferences

The root of the problem in describing values is to demonstrate the operation of consistent behavioral preferences. Irwin (1961) defines preference in the statement: "An organism . . . prefers one outcome of its behavior to another if and only if its choice among alternative acts depends upon the occurrence of the one outcome rather than the other" (p. 293). In a typical preference experiment, an organism is presented with a set of possible goal objects over a series of trials in which the spatial position and other secondary characteristics of the choice objects are counterbalanced or controlled. Deutsch and Jones (1960) report an example of such an experiment in which rats preferred pure water to a weak salt solution. Young (1955) has developed an enormous amount of information on such preference patterns (and resultant value hierarchies) in many organisms under different circumstances.

Limitations in Our Treatment of Values

The psychology of motivation has conventionally included two major problems—*activation, or arousal,* and *direction.* Activation refers to the general level of energy displayed by an organism, and the problem is to account for variations in levels of activity. Direction refers to the selectivity of an organism's behavior—the discrimination of preferences—and the problem is to determine why organisms display certain preferences. General arousal and activation have received much attention in recent years, especially from physiological psychologists (see Lindsley, 1957; Malmo, 1959). The level of behavioral activity has been related with some success to the operation of particular neural structures, particularly the reticular formation of the brainstem. But the problem of "general motivation" is not central to the problem of values. Values are indicated by preferences as exhibited by selective behavior. Obviously, some level of activation is necessary for the operation of preferences—sleeping organisms don't choose. However, for purposes of this discussion, the varying levels of arousal are not important. We will assume that preferences are made generally within a moderate range of activation. Extreme states of stress, seizures, coma, and depression will be excluded from the discussion for the sake of convenience.[1]

[1] As Kelly (1958) pointed out, the assertion that the organism is *living* entails some degree of general motivation. Therefore, the mere assumption of some kind of "psychic energy" is completely gratuitous. However, the differences in the extent to which an organism is "living" (level of activation) remain quite relevant psychologically. Preference patterns are undoubtedly related to general activation level.

Another limitation we will work under may be clarified by considering a distinction proposed by the philosopher, R. S. Peters (1958), between "caused" and "reasoned" behaviors. Behavior that has a "reason" is purposive, goal-directed, and rule-following. To inquire about a reason is to ask what a person is up to, what he is trying to obtain, or attain. For example, a stunt man may purposely fall off a horse to show that it can be done safely, to comply with a director's instructions, or to practice falling. These reasons also represent values. The same act, however, may be "caused" instead of reasoned. A man may fall off a horse because of inexperience, because the horse bucked, or because the saddle slipped. Causes "happen" to a person. The resultant actions are not produced by purposive decision, but follow from environmental circumstances and the more or less automatic reflex characteristics of the human body. Caused behaviors, then, are outside the scope of the present treatment.

These two limitations—only moderate activation levels and only reasoned behavior—are mutually consistent. Behavior under stress, panic, or seizure conditions, or under sleeping, comatose, or tranquilized conditions—all of which do not generally occur at moderate activation levels or by reason—cannot be appropriately analyzed in terms of beliefs and values. Tolman (1932) made the same kind of disclaimer, considering his theoretical constructions on purposive behavior to be applicable only to "docile" organisms. By docility he meant a moderate level of activation and arousal.

This way of distinguishing purposive behavior does not solely depend upon introspective reports. Tolman's subjects were rats, and for them this possibility was precluded. For human beings, values—or reasons—may be inferred from actions. However, a person's stated reasons for his behavior, which Peters calls "*his*" reason," may or may not coincide with the reasons an observer would infer, which Peters calls "*the* reason." This distinction points to a complex aspect of human behavior—namely, that human beings frequently have an interest in saying they are up to one thing when they are really up to something else. Therefore, an analysis of behaviorally operative values must not be exclusively dependent upon self-report data.

The Lessons from Freud—Pros and Cons

One of Sigmund Freud's great contributions to psychology concerned this issue. He discovered that a deep, thorough, and creatively reconstructive analysis of a person's thought patterns revealed startling inconsistencies of which the person did not seem to be aware (see Hall, 1954). One aim of psychoanalytic therapy is to uncover reasons for the inappropriate, incapacitating, or embarrassing behaviors that make a person seem "neurotic." In effect, Freud's explorations led him to construct a new theoretical psychological world, with three psychic compartments—the id, the ego, and the superego—a split between "the unconscious" and "the conscious," and two sovereign motives—sex and aggression. This is the kind of inner construction of mind that seemed demanded by Freud's clinical observations, and in effect, it provided a framework within which neurotic behavior seemed quite reasonable.

For our purposes, Freud's main contributions were, (1) demonstrating that stated reasons for behavior are reinterpretable—that convincing underlying consistencies can be discovered in apparent contradictions—and (2) revealing the dynamic complexity of psychological functioning. However, as a whole, the theoretical structure that Freud created has been unconvincing to many psychologists (see Jastrow, 1932; Rachman, 1963).[2] The difficulty with psychoanalytic theory is that it leads to thinking in terms of a conscious-unconscious split. Although Freud showed the importance of values in a system of psychology, he pushed all values into a mythic psychological underground. At best, this is an arbitrary way to think about values, and at worst it is completely defeating, for it assigns the formation of values to vaguely unconscious forces that only psychoanalytic procedures can bring into dubious light. The unreliability of verbal report and the possibility of reinterpreting the values behind behaviors are well accepted, but the accompanying substantive constructions of psychoanalytic theory are considered—at least here—as gratuitous and unnecessary for a discussion of values.

Situational Variation of Values: Values as a Product of Interaction

There is a temptation to think of values in substantive terms. The same problem was encountered with beliefs, and basically, the solution is the same. Values do not reside either in external objects or within the person; rather, they emerge from the interaction between a particular person and a particular portion of the environment. They are not objects of direct observation. In keeping with the preference paradigm outlined above, a statement of the values operating in any particular situation derives from observations of the *process of evaluation*.

Lewin (1936) suggested that the attractive force between a person and a region of the environment is related to the distance separating

[2] "Like most theories of our time, psychoanalysis, as a theory, was conceived as an absolute truth, and moreover, it was designed in such a manner that it tended to defy both logical examination and experimental validation. As the years go by, Freudianism, which deserved to be remembered as a brave outpost on the early frontier of psychological thought, is condemned to end its days as a crumbling stockade of proprietary dogmatism. Thus, as with other farseeing claims to absolute truth, history will have a difficult time deciding whether Freudianism did more to accelerate psychological progress during the first half of the twentieth century than it did to impede progress during the last half" (Kelly, 1958, p. 34).

these two entities. This is one example of how values may depend upon the situation. Miller (1959) has extended Lewin's idea and conceptualized it in terms of S-R theory to provide a general principle of conflict. He used a goal gradient to represent the increase in saliency of goal objects (either positive or negative) with proximity. The principle is well supported, at least by research done with rats, children, and college sophomores. Rats pull harder on a harness the nearer they are to a positive stimulus (food). The negative force of an aversive stimulus is similarly related to proximity. In this conceptualization, distance is liberalized to include dimensions of meaning and symbolism. Thus, a child may react to a doll as a symbolic representation of its mother, but the reactions may be much stronger when the mother is actually present.

Some work has also been done to determine the extent to which values expressed in one setting can be generalized to other settings. It has been shown that responses to stimulus objects display gradients of generalization. Thus, a child may show signs of fear and repulsion when presented with a stimulus object that resembles an object previously associated with pain. In Watson's (1928) classic demonstration, a little boy showed a generalized fear of small white animals after an unpleasant experience in the presence of one.

Goal gradients of this sort lead to changes in values over situations. A person may not feel like swimming until he passes by the beach and sees the water. In a real sense, his operative values have changed according to the proximity of the goal stimulus.

An even simpler sort of dependency between the situation and expressed values can be traced to situational constraints on the expression of values. For example, in the Deutsch and Jones (1960) experiment, rats preferred to drink pure water rather than a weak salt solution. However, if given the chance, they might have preferred an alcohol solution to either alternative.[3] Similarly, in the summertime a person may find little opportunity to express a high value for skiing, and schoolchildren may prefer to study geography rather than arithmetic only because the opportunity for recess is denied them. In sum, exhibited preferences are always limited by the range of alternatives present in the situation and may not be generalizable to situations containing different options or constraints. These options or constraints may derive from the fixed ideas of an interrogator as well as the physical limitations of choice. For example, if the behavior analyst is convinced that all behavior derives from either sex or aggression, his subject or client, who thinks he has an intrinsic liking for gardening or soap-carving, may be in a real dilemma.

[3] This touches upon a matter that has been relatively neglected in research on values but that may be potentially important—namely, the genetic determination of values. McClearn and Rogers (1961), for example, have demonstrated widely different preference patterns for alcohol consumption in mice of different species. While a great deal of work remains to be done on this problem, there seems ample documentation of the possibility that predisposition for certain preferences is inborn.

Ecological variations are not the only source of complication in the generalizability of values. Personal (internal) variation over time is another. For example, the value of food is related to the time lapse since the last meal. During World War II, a group of conscientious objectors agreed to undergo a period of experimental starvation (Brozek, Guetzkow, & Baldwin, 1951). During the latter stages of the experiment, all value objects other than food seemed highly irrelevant. Similarly, in the Old Testament story of Jacob and Esau, Esau came from the field faint with hunger and sold Jacob his birthright for a batch of lentil pottage.

There are intricacies in the determination of values beyond personal and situational constraints. Lewin suggested that under certain circumstances objects that are difficult to attain are thereby more highly valued than easily obtainable objects. More recently, Lawrence and Festinger (1962) have provided experimental evidence that the extent to which the fruits of hard work are appreciated (valued) depends upon how hard the work was. Lewis (1965) has provided further evidence on the complicated relationship between amount of work and incentive value. The value of an object depends not only on its desirability to the individual and its worth on the open market, but also on how it was come by.

In sum, any statement about values points in two directions—toward a person and toward a valued event, object, or state of being. Values are contextual occurrences in that they depend upon a variety of internal conditions, external stimulus configurations, and response options. They are relational in that they represent a relationship between the valuing person and the valued object. Thus, values inhere neither in persons nor in objects, events, or states of being. They emerge, rather, from the interaction or commerce between the person and his psychological ecology.

VALUE CATALOGS

Listing of Values

The construction of value lists can now be considered from the preceding perspective. Generally, these lists are of two types, depending upon whether the referent is considered to be internal (personal) or external (ecological). Lists of motives are examples of the internal type, and lists of prices are examples of the external type.

Price lists are catalogs of objects, in which names or other symbolic representations are paired with numbers that represent the worth or value of the objects. Motive or need lists, on the other hand, are not catalogs of objects but rather of presumed personal dispositions. In this case the pairings are between labels—such as "need for autonomy," "anxiety level," or "aggressivity"—and numbers, or quasi-quantitative statements, which are meant to represent the strengths of corresponding internal tendencies. In making a catalog, two major problems must be solved: (1) organizing a system of categories to which symbolic labels can be affixed and (2) assigning values to the established categories.

Categorizing objects in merchandizing is a matter of establishing convenient conventions. A set of wrenches may be listed as a set, or listed wrench by wrench. Nails and screws may be sold by weight, volume, or number. A set of books may be priced according to a number of options—with or without a bookcase, with or without buckram covers, and so on. In some cases the arbitrariness of pricing categories produces inequities, as when a balding man is charged as much for a haircut as a mop-headed college sophomore. Obviously, there is no single "right" way to prepare a list of merchandise, for a convention that is convenient under some circumstances may not remain convenient if circumstances change. Cake mixes, for example, are essentially a recategorization (with corresponding repackaging) of commodities already available to the housewife. As the resources and conditions of the housewife change, merchandising categories are modified to suit the new circumstances.

Pricing, of course, is a complex process of assessing the willingness of the consumer to part with units of money in exchange for a commodity. It is apparent to students of economics, or to travelers, that the factors that influence pricing are multiple—that supply and demand serve only as collective labels for a multitude of influences, such as perishability, transportation facilities, styles, tightness of credit, similarity to other available goods, and so on. It is meaningless to talk in absolute and universal terms about the price of anything, for prices—like systems of commodity listing and organization—are influenced by changing circumstances.

Lists of psychological needs or motives must also be organized, classified, and categorized. A definitive catalog of human values has been a central preoccupation throughout the history of psychology. Despite an enormous variety of general names for items in the list (for example, instincts, faculties, needs, motives, traits, or primary drives), there are common ways of going about the task, and the lists that emerge are similar in many respects.

The Tradition of "Psychological Faculties"

In 1821 a movement started in Europe that was a natural outgrowth of the faculty psychologies of the ancients. It was called the "science" of phrenology. The founder of the movement, Gall, and his disciple, Spurzheim, dedicated themselves to identifying and quantifying the basic human faculties by minutely examining the conformations of the human skull. They believed that outstanding personal traits or characteristics are expressed in protuberances of the skull.[4]

---

[4] The ease with which phrenology may be criticized has prompted some writers to note positive accomplishments of the movement, among which are (a) the adoption

The phrenologists' procedure was to examine the prominent cranial features of individuals known to be exceptional in some aspect of life—such as respected judges, habitual criminals, devoted mothers, and outstanding athletes. From this data, they produced lists of traits with accompanying cranial maps that could be employed to assess an individual's psychological make-up. Included was a list of human propensities and sentiments—effectively, a list of values. Desire to live, destructiveness, amativeness, benevolence, firmness, ideality, and mirthfulness are examples of items in this list.

Later in the nineteenth century, Darwin's theory of continuity among life forms renewed interest in the question of human instincts. Attempts were made to develop lists of instincts, each containing a different number of instincts and different criteria by which specific instincts were admitted. Although there were disputes as to whether instincts were modifiable, whether they had cognitive content, and whether individual members of species could differ in the amount of an instinct carried, there was general agreement that instincts were *inborn values*.

The concept of instinct in animals serves as an explanation of the natural attraction of certain species for certain features of the environment. Insects, for example, seem to be born with preferences for specific foods, climates, and habitats. The procedure for describing human instincts derived from a similar explanatory necessity. Basically, the task was to generalize the kinds of things that men seem disposed to approach or avoid.

Understandably, the contents of resultant lists varied considerably. McDougall (1908) composed a list of 21 instincts and included such items as flight, repulsion, curiosity, pugnacity, and the parental instinct. James (1890) devised a list of indefinite length because some instincts were labeled partial or special. He included jealousy, play, cleanliness, sociability, and sympathy.

Early in his writings, Freud (1950b) took a different view, hypothesizing a single and sovereign life value in pansexual libidinal energy. In a later work (Freud, 1950a), he felt it necessary to hypothesize an opposing set of instincts—death instincts. According to this formulation, everything that man does may be seen as either constructive or destructive, corresponding to the opposed metabolic processes of anabolism and catabolism. Thus, all values derive ultimately from either the forces of life or the forces of death.

McCall (1963) provides a more modern version of value listing. He defines a motive as a "felt tendency respecting the cognized desirable-undesirable" (p. 289) and lists four categorical biological motives: hunger,

---

of an empirical method, (b) the stimulation of interest in localization of brain function, and (c) the final establishment of the head as the locus of mental functioning after centuries of dispute about where thinking takes place (see Boring, 1957; Allport, 1937; Krech, 1962).

thirst, and excretory drive, and the rest-or-sleep drive. In addition, he notes several "preemptive" motives, among which are pain avoidance, activity, and sex.

Psychological literature abounds with catalogues of human instincts. Spranger (1928) listed six basic human types according to the ascendancy of particular constellations of values. The types are: Theoretic, Aesthetic, Political, Religious, Social, and Practical. In a recent study of values in college students, Scott (1965) included kindness, physical development, self-control, and creativity in his list of 12 values. Murray (1938) established a list of 20 psychological needs, including the need for achievement, the need for exhibition, and the need for order.

Once a list of values (motives, needs, faculties, or instincts) is established, the other half of the task—assessing the amount of each value possessed by an individual—still remains. Psychologists have developed an intricate technology on this problem. The basic devices are the interview and the psychological test, which presume to reflect the quantity of each value possessed by the respondent. For Freudian needs there is the Blacky Test by Blum (1950); for Spranger's six types of values there is the Allport, Vernon, and Lindzey (1951) *Study of Values*, and for Murray's list of needs there is his own Thematic Apperception Test (Murray, 1943) and the Edwards Personal Preference Schedule (Edwards, 1954).

Although each of these instruments has been shown to have a limited practical utility, the mere number and variety of value catalogs pose a theoretical problem for the psychology of values. Diversity is to be expected in the case of mercantile catalogs, in which systems of categorization and setting of prices are arbitrary. But if we take differences in catalogs as evidence of arbitrariness, the evidence is also ample that lists of personal values are no less arbitrary. Unfortunately, many authors of such lists do not share this view, but consider their particular lists to be somehow exhaustive and uniquely correct.[5] Boring (1957) noted that instinct psychology fell into disrepute when "psychologists discovered that anyone can make up his own list of instincts and there is no way to prove that one list is more certainly correct than another" (p. 718). Yet this lesson has not yet dissuaded those who would try to formulate *the definitive* list of human values.[6]

The difficulty is that personal value catalogs are often considered not as mere descriptions of values but as explanations of behavior. Varia-

[5] Some authors are more modest, however, James (1890) offers his doubts in a footnote to his chapter on instincts: "With the boundaries of instinct fading into reflex action below and into acquired habit or suggested activity above, it is likely that there will always be controversy about just what to include under the class name. Shall we add the propensity to walk along a curbstone, or any other narrow path, to the list of instincts? Shall we subtract secretiveness, as due to shyness of to fear? Who knows?" (p. 440).

[6] See Rotter (1954) for a thorough critique of trait, type, and faculty theories

tions in descriptions of human values need not be too distressing, for descriptions are dependent upon the cognitive predispositions of the beholder (see Chapter II). But if man's behavior is to be explained by a list of personal values, then the wide variation in these lists is troubling. We can envision a possibility parallel to the wide variation of causes attributed to behavioral deviation, as noted in Chapter II. For example, why did Michelangelo paint the ceiling of the Sistine Chapel? Did his efforts derive from the economic motive? From the need for creativity? From the artistic value? As a sublimation and indirect expression of the libidinal sexual instinct? From the religious motive? From the expressive instinct? The possibilities could be extended *ad nauseum*.

The two types of value catalog—price lists and motive lists—seem equally unstable, and if anything, price lists are probably more strongly predictive of behavior than motive lists. Traditionally, economists have been concerned with price lists, and psychologists with motive lists. It should be apparent, however, that both types of lists are psycho-economic, or eco-psychologic. Through historical accident and professional provincialism, price lists and motive lists have been considered as completely different kinds of things. But the assertion here, following from the view that all values are bi-directional or interactive, is that these two types of lists are variations of a single kind. Each is a limited and conditional statement of transactional tendencies under circumscribed conditions.

Values and Explanations

The operations of preference used to define values do not, in themselves, *explain* any behavior. Once values are determined by observing preference operations, however, they may be used to make behavioral predictions and thus may enter into explanations. For example, we may predict, on the basis of Deutsch's experiment, that rats will learn a task faster with pure water than with a weak salt solution as reward. Therefore, it might be said that a difference in learning speed is due to the difference in the reward values of the two substances.

Similarly, instincts, needs, or motives cannot serve as explanations of the very observations by which they were defined. Motive lists, and especially lists of instincts, frequently lead to the *nominal fallacy*—that is, considering a phenomenon explained when it is merely named (Beach, 1955). Does a person hoard money? The avarice instinct is strong in him. Does a person eat too much? The hunger instinct is out of balance. Similarly, referring to a high "anxiety level" as the cause of erratic behavior is little more than redescribing the behavior in metaphorical terms.[7] But avarice, hunger, and anxiety level could be used to make predictions

[7] Sarbin (1964, 1967b) has presented a convincing case that anxiety is a psychological metaphor that has outlived its usefulness because it is often used in a pseudo-

about behaviors other than those described by the labels themselves. The utility of these value labels is then properly reduced to the practical and empirical level.

THE ORIGINS OF VALUES

The Derivation of Values and the Question of Preemptiveness

A distinction is customarily made between basic or primary values and derived or secondary values. Originally unvalued items may become valued by association with items that are already valued. Western culture is especially rich in a genre of objects known as souvenirs—otherwise worthless trifles that have acquired value by association with valued persons, places, or events. Money is perhaps the most common example of a valued object whose worth is only in relationship to other objects. The difference in the two examples is that money is instrumental to the attainment of other valued commodities, whereas souvenirs are merely evocative of pleasure in an idiosyncratic manner. Parallel examples are a can opener, which has instrumental value, versus an oil painting, which has evocative or representational value. Objects may have both instrumental and representational secondary value, as in the case of postage stamps and coins.

In psychology, the major vehicle for explaining the operation of the process of value contagion has been the conditioning paradigm. An initially meaningless signal or stimulus, when paired with some direct satisfaction, comes to evoke a response similar to that evoked by the direct satisfaction. Conditioning is of two major kinds—classical and instrumental. In classical conditioning, satisfaction is either given or withheld independently of the organism's behavior—neither the originally meaningless stimulus object nor the organism's actions produce the satisfaction. An example of classical conditioning is Pavlov's experiments with dogs, in which the animals learned to respond to a bell in a way that partially resembled their natural response to food powder. In instrumental conditioning, either the stimulus object or some behavior of the organism directly produces the satisfaction. For example, chimpanzees can learn to put tokens in a vending machine in order to obtain food (Wolff, 1936). The value of the tokens is then instrumental. Souvenirs fit the classical conditioning paradigm, whereas money fits the instrumental.

explanatory fashion. "For nearly half a century, a romantic mystique has evolved around the professional enterprise stimulated by Freud's colorful metaphors (one of which is 'anxiety'). Experienced clinicians recognize that the mystique is not justified—and that when therapy is successful, it is not due to the purging of anxiety. Rather, it is because the patient has learned how to minimize, with his finite cognitive capacities, the strains produced in his efforts to find himself in a complex, changing and often contradictory world" (1964, p. 638).

It is not necessary to elaborate on the large number of theoretical mechanisms that have been invented by psychologists to account for the generalization of values. What must be recognized is that the demonstration that values give rise to other values does not solve the problem of identifying the "basic human motives." Unfortunately, psychologists have often been content to demonstrate one or two such value derivations and then, by analogy, to explain the whole range of human values in terms of the illustrated paradigm.

The word "primary" in the phrase "primary value" may be interpreted in several ways. It may mean "inherited and universally present in all members of a species"—as are hunger and thirst. Or it may refer to the order of derivation between two valued events. For example, the primary objective of winning a race imparts value to the secondary objective of training. Finally, it may refer to the preemptive or prerequisite character of some values. To aspire to be a philosopher, according to Plato, one must first have enough to eat.

This last interpretation concerning priority has suggested a somewhat different idea of the development of human values than the simple conditioning paradigm. Maslow (1954) hypothesized a natural hierarchy of human motives, with fundamental needs like eating, safety, and shelter at the base of the hierarchy, and expressive, esthetic, "self-actualizing" needs at the top. According to Maslow, there is a dependency among levels of this hierarchy, but it is not one of contagion. The satisfaction of more fundamental needs "releases" a person to strive for the satisfaction of higher-order needs. For Maslow, creative efforts are not seen as a sublimation or substitution of goal objects from a common value, but as spontaneously emerging and *intrinsically valuable* activities.

The specific content of Maslow's motivational hierarchy is not as important as is his argument that higher-order values may emerge spontaneously in a manner that makes them essentially irreducible to more fundamental values.[8] In the next section we will consider some evidence for this possibility.

Intrinsic Motivation: Values Are Where You Find Them

The dominant psychological thought in the first half of the twentieth century favored an adjustment or tension-reduction origin of values. The principle of homeostasis (Cannon, 1932) was most commonly employed to explain how certain goals and instrumental behaviors have intrinsic

[8] Allport (1937) introduced the concept of "functional autonomy" to describe cases in which originally derived values acquire and sustain an independent, intrinsic value. For example, a person may strive for money merely to accumulate it rather than to use it to gain a more primary satisfaction (food). In this case, the value of striving for money has become functionally autonomous. Seward (1963) has provided a very useful discussion of the current status of this conception.

value for the organism. In this conception, the organism is viewed as a semicontained energy system requiring certain amounts of nutrient substances and certain levels of favorable environmental conditions. When, for example, the glucose concentration of the blood falls below a certain level, eating behavior is instigated until a feedback signal from the stomach indicates that sufficient food has been ingested (see Rosenzweig, 1962). The body has similar regulatory mechanisms for temperature, water balance, blood saline concentration, and density of red blood cells. The classical position is that only those objects and behaviors that directly relate to the body's equilibrium-maintaining mechanisms have primary or intrinsic value.

This same model was employed by Freud, only in his case a metaphorical psychic energy (deriving from the id) was considered the source of psychic tension. The building up of this "substance," in turn, leads to attempts to relieve the tension—directly if possible, or indirectly if necessary (because of counterpressures of the ego and superego). If too much tension builds up, the psychic apparatus becomes functionally disrupted, and symptom formation results.

This conception of intrinsic values, allied with the value-contagion principles noted in the previous section, produces a nicely parsimonious conception of the origin and nature of human values. The problem is that the conception is too parsimonious, for the wide array of operative human values includes many that can only be accommodated by a Procrustean tailoring of the facts.

An important discovery in modern psychological research is that "pleasure areas" exist in the brain, both in lower animals (Olds, 1955) and in man (Heath, 1963). Very slight electrical stimulation administered to certain areas of the brain through surgically placed electrodes produces unmistakable signs of pleasure. Rats learn to press a lever repeatedly to obtain such stimulation, and can even learn a difficult maze receiving only a small electrical jolt as reward. Human subjects who have been stimulated in the "pleasure areas" of the brain during brain surgery report feelings of positive affect and euphoria. In terms of the preference paradigm, electrical stimulation of these areas functions as a value. Yet no obvious tension is reduced by brain stimulation; if anything, excitation in the brain is increased. And such stimulation appears to serve no function in the regulation and adjustment of optimal living conditions. Indeed, rats have been shown to prefer direct electrical stimulation to eating, and have suffered for the preference.

Other evidence also points to the limited usefulness of the tension-reduction concept. Montgomery (1953) has shown that rats show distinct preferences for the exploration (without food reward) of certain types of mazes. Berlyne (1960) has produced a great deal of evidence on the intrinsic values of exploration and novelty. Harlow's (1958) observations of "mother love" in young monkeys indicate that they tend to prefer certain tactual and visual cues from mother substitutes, and that these preferences are not derived from the nurturant capacities of the mother substitute. Butler (1953) has shown that monkeys solve complex mechanical puzzles for the pleasure of opening a little door and looking out of their compartment, perhaps to see a chugging electric train. White (1959), after summarizing the evidence against a simple tension-reduction model, concluded that there are grounds for supposing "competence" and "effectance" to be intrinsic rewards for a variety of species. Maslow's theory about the spontaneous emergence of higher-order intrinsic values has already been noted; it is certainly consistent with the evidence just quoted (see also, Seward, 1963).

The reply of those who would maintain that all intrinsic values are related to adjustment and survival potential is that certain values relate not to survival of the individual but to survival of the species. Indeed, the evolutionary argument is antecedent to the development of both homeostatic principle and Freud's dynamic psychology. The value of sex (which could be quoted as contrary to the tension-reduction model since sexual *excitation* is normally construed as pleasurable), for example, may be seen as contributing to the survival ability not of the individual but of the species. Therefore, sex is functional in an evolutionary rather than an individual sense. Similarly, competence, effectance, exploration, and even a sense of justice and ethics may be seen as direct manifestations of survival necessities for the species.

The geneticist, Waddington, has stated that "the framework within which one can carry on a rational discussion of different systems of ethics, and make comparisons of their various merits and demerits, is to be found in a consideration of animal and human evolution" (quoted in Dobzhansky, 1962, p. 343). This position suggests that all values, including higher-order ethical principles, are a product of biological evolution and are direct reflections of the values of survival and continued evolution, which are ipso facto valuable processes. Dobzhansky (1962), also a geneticist, says that this solution is too easy, pointing out that we don't always know what is and what is not in step with nature. Cultural evolution is different from biological evolution, and has produced so wide a range of values that "natural values" are a matter of irresolvable dispute. The natural ethical consequences of social Darwinism (see Chapter I) seemed quite unnatural to many moralists. "Human values and wisdom are products of cultural evolution, conditioned of course by biological evolution, yet not deducible from the latter. In point of fact, man will not be dissuaded from the arrogant aspiration to query whether the biological and cosmic evolutions, which produced him among countless other things, do or do not conform to his wisdom and values" (Dobzhansky, 1962, p. 345).

Arguments have been made for a utilitarian or functionalist view of art, magic, and religion. In general, the arguments consider that these enterprises increase the biological fitness of man as a species. Indeed, an argument will be presented in Chapter VI that superstitions have a positive functional significance. But note that these categories—art, religion, superstition, and so on—are quite general and subsume different values in different cultures. The proposal here is that man has been prepared through evolution to accept certain general kinds of values, but that evolution has not determined what the precise content of those values should be.

Cultural variation in values is obvious. The Japanese eat raw fish, but North Americans are repulsed by the very idea. Moslems have many wives, and Christians are generally monogamous. In Brazil, it is disgraceful to be ill with tuberculosis but not socially disastrous to contract venereal disease (Freyre, 1956). Certain Eskimo tribes practice euthanasia, which other cultures consider murder. The only way to determine the nature of values within a culture is to make a direct assessment of that culture. There are, of course, universals of value as well as universals of language. Osgood (1966) has shown that a number of descriptive adjectives are regarded as evaluatively positive over cultures (for example, good, sweet, smooth, up, bright, white). Whether cultural differences are more important than similarities is a moot and value-laden question. Further, no theory of values has ever been able to explain the origin of values so as to account for their sheer number and variety. Any such theory would ultimately have to contend with the mechanics of enculturation, a process that is itself not well understood.

Fortunately, the origin of values does not need to be theoretically deduced in order for the values themselves to be measurable and operational psychological variables. For the present, it is sufficient to take values where and as they are found, without attempting to trace their primitive origins. In this sense, the constructions of instinct lists were positive steps, except for the unfortunate tendency to explain a class of behaviors by merely naming the class. Value lists are a crucial component of the analysis of any behavioral problem, whether it involves individuals or collectivities such as nations or cultures.

UTILITY

The Economic View of Value

The concept of utility was created out of a recognition that the psychological or subjective value of money may not be the same as its apparent or numerical value. A prize of $50, for example, would not necessarily make a person exactly one-half as happy as a prize of $100.

Utility, therefore, is simply subjective value, scaled in units called *utiles* as money is scaled in dollars or pounds. Nothing in the notion of utility indicates what kinds of things or events should or should not be valued subjectively. We merely assume—as we did in the previous section—that values exist where they exist.

A major problem with utility theory concerns how utilities can be assessed in a generalizable way. The basic operation of assessment is always a preference judgment among a set of presented options—essentially the same preference operation so frequently referred to in this chapter. Generalizability, in this sense, is the potential to make inferences about the difference in utility between, for example, $500 and $1000, on the basis of information obtained on the differences in utility between $50 and $100.

Utility scaling faces essentially the same problems as psychophysical scaling (at least where a monetary scale is a reference). Just as the psychological dimensions of loudness and luminosity do not correspond perfectly (linearly) to the physical dimensions of amplitude and physical intensity (albedo), so does utility fail to correspond perfectly to the dimension of monetary value. The task is to describe a general function relating the psychological dimension to the physical.[9]

One complication is that many valued objects and conditions do not bear price tags. In deciding whether or not to take Botany 101, for example, various sources of utility may be involved: the value of being in the same class as the attractive Miss X; the price of the text and required equipment; the hour the class meets; the distance to and from the classroom; the usefulness of botanical knowledge in later life; the relation of the course to degree requirements; and so on. It is difficult to place a price tag on some of the obviously valuable factors. Formally, this is known as the problem of multidimensional utility. Practically, the problem is to reduce the many value considerations to a single index of utility.

A closely related problem concerns exchange rates between commodities. In economy with limited productive resources, increments in the production of one commodity must be offset by decrements in the production of another. If the only two items produced are guns and butter, production of more guns forces production of less butter. This means that some function relating gun utility to butter utility must be created. Similarly, there must be some function relating human lives to dollars spent. In fighting wars, building bridges, testing aircraft, and exploring space, it is necessary to consider that lives will be lost and that addi-

[9] See Edwards, Lindman, and Phillips (1965) for a useful introduction to utility theory. These authors note that Gustave Fechner, who is known as the father of psychophysics, was inspired by the earlier work of Daniel Bernoulli on the problem of utility.

tional time and money spent on safety precautions can reduce the number.

Exchange functions between commodities (or events, lives, or states of being—regarded as commodities) are not constant over individuals or situations. Thus, the additional complications of situational and personal specificity are introduced. For example, the value of a human life during wartime depends upon whose life it is (a general, one of his soldiers, one of the enemy) and the conditions under which it might be lost (in battle, in a hospital, during training).

Despite the apparent absurdity of trying to relate the value of guns to butter, to lives, to political advantage, to comfort, and so on, there is ample evidence that such judgments are made. Indeed, life seems to require them rather frequently. Decisions must be made—whether or not to take Botany 101, to build a bridge, to drop a bomb, to go to the moon, to try income tax evasion, to take LSD, or to marry.

By asking for just such absurd judgments in the laboratory, psychologists have been able to develop some interesting and predictively useful results. Galanter (1962), for example, determined that the amount of money that had twice as much utility as $10 was on the average $53; for twice as much utility as $1000, subjects wanted an average of $10,220. Becker and Siegel (1958) determined the utility scale underlying the academic grade scale, and found that the distance between A and B for many students was less than the distance between B and C, and that the distances depended regularly on how good the students were. In both of these cases, the experimental procedure was simply to obtain hypothetical judgments from subjects on questions such as, "How much money would make you feel twice as happy as $10 would make you feel?" and, "Would you prefer a 50-50 chance of an A or a C to a certain B?"

To explore the way a person makes utility judgments and to examine his exchange functions (for example, how much he is willing to sacrifice to become a doctor) is to explore his values. It bears repeating that such explorations always have situational limitations. If a person is asked whether he would prefer to go bowling or to kiss girls, he may give an answer that differs from his actual behavior when he is presented with this choice. Nonetheless, the Strong Vocational Interest Blank, which is a large-scale inventory of preference judgments, is a good predictor of real-life career decisions (Strong, 1955). The theory behind this instrument is simple. A person has distinct interests and is likely to enter into professions characterized by similar interests. A sample item from the Strong test is given below. The utility judgments required are obviously complex; yet they can be performed, and the information they contain is of considerable behavioral importance.

Order of Preferred Activities. Here are ten things you could do. First read all ten. Then pick out three of them, the three things you think you would like best to do. Check these three items in column 1. Then select the three things you would like least to do, and show which they are by marking in column 3. Then mark the remaining four items in the middle column where no marks have been made so far.

1 2 3

— — — Develop the theory of operation of a new machine. e.g., auto
— — — Operate (manipulate) the new machine
— — — Discover an improvement in the design of the machine
— — — Determine the cost of operation of the machine
— — — Supervise the manufacture of the machine
— — — Create a new artistic effect, i.e., improve the beauty of the auto
— — — Sell the machine
— — — Prepare the advertising for the machine
— — — Teach others the use of the machine
— — — Interest the public in the machine through public addresses

The Utility of "Finding Out" and Other Hidden Values

As was pointed out before, many organisms display what appears to be intrinsic exploratory behavior. If exploration is looked upon as acquiring knowledge, or beliefs about what leads to what, then beliefs have utility. Indeed, it should be obvious from fhe last chapter that this is so. Without beliefs, intelligent behavior in a complex environment would be impossible.

This "natural" tendency to explore the environment seems coupled in man with a "natural" inclination to organize what he sees. Royce (1894) states that if a man is placed "in a perfect chaos of phenomena, sights, sounds, feelings; . . . if the man continued to exist, and to be rational at all, his attention would doubtless soon find for him a way to make up some kind of rhythmic regularity, which he would impute to the things about him, so as to imagine that he had discovered some law of sequence in this mad new world" (p. 317).

Earlier in this chapter the assertion was made that the prescription of absolute values is not the objective of science—its business is fact. This assertion does not mean that science has nothing to do with values, especially of the moral ("ought") kind. Like any other complex human enterprise, science is loaded with values—preferences translated into utilities—and very likely one of its major values is the intrinsic desire to explore and organize apparent chaos.

Other values that are inherent in the scientific enterprise are not as obvious. Science has produced technology, and technology produces rapid cultural change, which in turn, is not evaluatively neutral. Many people see man dehumanized and degraded as the machine assumes supremacy in the world (see Wiener, 1964; Handlin, 1964). Science, after all, has produced "the bomb," and such a force has profound effects on the evolution of human values. Do scientists implement their own values in helping to bring about these changes?[10]

The area of psychodiagnosis presents a similar problem. Sarbin (1967b) has cogently argued that diagnoses of mental illness are not applications of some clear definition of sickness and health, but manifestations of the diagnostician's values. Agents of society commonly administer sanctions for deviant behavior, but the difficulty with mental illness is that the official set of value judgments about proper human behavior is rarely recognized as a set of value judgments. Instead, criteria of mental illness are cast in the form of elliptical scientific propositions, which do not seem evaluative. Rotter (1963) has stated that "with the exception of Rogers and some of the followers of Adler, most clinical psychologists have avoided the problem of defining their own values. Instead, they rely on the concept of disease borrowed from medicine. By some ultimate criterion not made explicit, specific behaviors or constellations of behaviors are indications of disease, and anyone having a specific disease needs treatment. Therefore, we have the illness of the psychopath, immature personality, nervous disposition, psychotic, compulsive neurotic and the rest. Diseases themselves are identified by authorities and may be found described in certain textbooks" (p. 280). In this manner, psychotherapists may be instrumental in bringing about changes that are merely applications of their own values, while they themselves believe they are performing scientific tasks.

Both in origin and effect, the work of the scientist—not just the psychologist and nuclear physicist, but also the geneticist, cell physiologist, and medical researcher—is strongly evaluative. Whitehead states this point well:

> Judgments of worth are no part of the texture of physical sciences, but they are part of the motive of its production. Mankind has raised the

---

[10] The following quotation from an article by Allport (1954) on the history of social psychology is illustrative of the value-laden character of scientific ideas: "The theories of social psychology are rarely, if ever, chaste scientific productions. They usually gear into the prevailing political and social atmosphere. Dewey . . . has shown that this is so. For example, an aristocracy produces no psychology of individual differences, for the individual is unimportant unless he happens to belong to the higher classes. Dewey likewise points out that dualistic psychology flourishes best when one group holds a monopoly of social power and wishes to do the thinking and planning, while others remain the docile, unthinking instruments of execution. And apologists for the status quo . . . are the ones who most readily declare human nature to be unalterable" (p. 11).

edifice of science, because they have judged it worthwhile. In other words, the motives involve innumerable judgments of value. Again, there has been conscious selection of the parts of the scientific fields to be cultivated and this conscious selection involved judgments of value. These values may be aesthetic or moral or utilitarian; namely, judgments as to the beauty of the structure or as to the duty of exploring the truth or as to utility in the satisfaction of physical wants. But whatever the motive, without judgments of value there could have been no science. (1929, p. 228)

SUMMARY

Preferences exhibited under moderate levels of activation, and not made under the influence of a debilitating external agent, are the reference observations for the inference of values. Inferences made from these observations, however, are complicated by the fact, which Freud pointed out, that more convincing value explanations can frequently be discovered after a more intensive inquiry is made. Value is also a bi-directional concept that points to both a valuing organism and a valued object. Since values inhere neither in persons nor in objects, changes in either the situation or the state of the person are likely to bring about changes in manifest orderings of values.

All lists of values are in essence the same—pairings of arbitrary class labels with arbitrarily determined value units (dollars, utiles, quantities of need, and so on). Traditionally, lists of prices and lists of motives have been the separate fields of economists and psychologists, respectively, but the present conception of values reveals a fundamental similarity in the motivational concerns of these disciplines.

Although the principles of homeostasis and simple conditioning have provided a simple working conception of the nature of primary values and their generalization to secondary objects, a number of observations lead to the conclusion that this view is both limited and unnecessary. The extension of the homeostatic view from the individual to the species tends to confuse biological evolution, which predisposes man to accept certain classes of values, and cultural evolution, which determines what these classes of values shall contain.

By developing the conception of utility, economists have recognized that value is a psychological problem. Utility functions, relating money to satisfaction or pleasure, and exchange functions, representing the value of one commodity with respect to another, represent an idealized or collective psychological condition. The utility concept eliminates a good deal of needless complexity on the question of values (the question of where utilities "come from" is excluded) but itself creates an interesting range of problems, including how disparate values combine in a single decision and how values depend on situational and personal changes.

The scientific procedure is a manifestation of collective value judgments. The danger, however, is that laymen and scientists alike do not often realize how values operate in science, and thus, may inadvertently leave to science the problem of deciding what is ultimately best for society. This issue raises the question of the value of developing beliefs out of uncertainty and creating order out of chaotic experience. The implication is that this value is strongly involved in scientific behavior. In the next chapter, the relation of beliefs and values to behavior is explored more systematically.

IV

The Behavioral Consequences of Beliefs and Values

We always move on two feet—the two poles of knowledge and
desire.   **Elie Faure**[1]

WE HAVE DEVELOPED the concepts of beliefs and values in order to
apply them to behavior. The proposition that beliefs and values determine
behavior was asserted in Chapter I, and it was implied in all that was said
in the subsequent two chapters. In this chapter, the relationship will be
spelled out in more detail.

SIMPLE DECISION PARADIGMS

As a start, consider two somewhat more explicit statements of the
relationship of beliefs and values to behavior: (1) If values are defined
and held constant, variations in behavior will correspond to variations
in expectancies. (2) Given equivalent expectancies associated with behavioral options, variations in behavior will correspond to variations in
value.

Quest

If behavior is a function of beliefs and values, then presumably
an individual who is obsessed by a single overriding value would direct
his behavior according to expectations about how that value might be
realized. Thus, Diogenes searching for an honest man, or Ponce de Leon
searching for the fountain of youth, or alchemists searching for an elixir,

[1] Quoted in Jastrow (1935), p. 1.

or a hunter looking for quail, or parents seeking a lost child would all presumably guide their behavior according to beliefs about what *might* lead to what—in other words, probabilistic expectancies. We could reasonably suppose that the a priori most likely locations of the target objects would be inspected first, followed by the next most likely, and so on, until searching became a matter either of random or systematic scanning, indicating that no differential expectancies existed regarding unexplored parts of the ecology. Systematic search strategies—such that each possible target location is inspected once and only once—are based on an expectation that such a procedure will most likely achieve the specified goal.

Omnipotence

The second paradigm is illustrated when anything conceivable is also possible or attainable. The clearest case is that of Superman of comic strip fame; but gods, very rich men, and presidents of giant corporations are useful approximations. Presumably, if a being can do absolutely anything, its behavior will follow directly from its values. Thus, Superman employs his powers to implement his conceptions of law and order (although he may gain a certain amount of secondary satisfaction out of cracking the heads of oafish criminal elements). Gods act in accord with their wills; they are usually not preoccupied with the uncertainty of their efforts. Similarly, the differences in life patterns among the very rich seem easily attributable to differences in values. Some prefer to live simply and to cultivate their intellects; others prefer to live conspicuously and to consume lavishly; still others disdain both intellectual preoccupations and lavish living in favor of building up greater reserves of wealth and power. The behavior of those who have access to great material resources seems to be a clear manifestion of values.

The More Common Case of Uncertainty and Ambiguity

Anyone who has looked for a pair of cufflinks (quest) or operated a multiple-choice vending machine (omnipotence—certainty of obtaining any objective in the setting) has conformed, if only for brief periods, with these paradigms of behavior. However, the more common case is one that is analytically more difficult, in which both beliefs and values are *variable* antecedents of behavior. Usually a person retains a margin of uncertainty about the possible results of his actions—he is not omnipotent. Moreover, the values associated with various types of outcomes are usually not equal or unequivocal. The behavioral outcomes in situations characterized by both uncertainty and ambivalence are not quite so obvious.

In order to formulate this relationship we must represent the basic concepts more concretely. A simple choice situation involving two alternatives, *A* and *B,* might be described as follows: Associated with each behavioral alternative is an expectancy of success and a complementary expectancy of failure. Associated with each possible outcome—both success and failure—is some amount of value. Thus, the problem of choosing between two possible $1 bets in a game of roulette might be represented as follows:

Alternative	Probability of Success	Value of Success	Probability of Failure	Value of Failure
A: Play black	$\frac{18}{38}$	+$ 1	$\frac{20}{38}$	−$1
B: Play #32	$\frac{1}{38}$	+$35	$\frac{37}{38}$	−$1

The numbers in this table are based on the standard rules for the game of roulette. A bet on the winning color wins an amount equal to the stake. The probability of winning on a color is the ratio of the number of possible outcomes of a given color (18) to the total number of possible outcomes (38 = 18 of each of two colors, plus two noncolored outcomes). The payoff for a bet on a single number is 35 times the amount bet. The probability that a given number will occur is $\frac{1}{38}$, since each of the 38 possible outcomes is considered to be equally likely.

The problem is to convert this information into a single prediction of behavior. For this purpose the concept of *Expected Value* must be introduced. Mathematically, the Expected Value is analogous to the arithmetic average of a series of scores or numbers. In the present case, the Expected Value of a bet could be estimated by averaging the wins and losses over a long series of plays on the same bet. Or, if the probabilities of each possible outcome are known, as well as the values of each of those outcomes, the Expected Value of a bet may be determined by a simple mathematical process. The probability of each outcome is multiplied by its associated value, and the resulting products are summed over each of the possible outcomes for a given alternative. The result is the Expected Value, which may be interpreted as the expected (average) amount of win or loss per play of a particular bet.

In the roulette example, the Expected Value of playing black (alternative A) is $(\frac{18}{38} \times \$1) + (\frac{20}{38} \times -\$1) = -.0525$ per play. The Expected Value of playing number 32 (alternative B) is similarly computed as $(\frac{1}{38} \times \$35) + (\frac{37}{38} \times -\$1) = -.0525$ per play. Thus, the Expected Values associated with playing black and playing number 32 are identical. Over the long run, a person would lose slightly more than a nickle per play for betting $1.00 on either one of these options. It follows that a person should be behaviorally neutral for these choice options—he should bet on black as often as on 32. Dozens of other bets in the game have exactly this Expected Value, and thus, they also should be played as often as either of the two bets discussed. However, we must also take into consideration another behavioral option that is always implicitly present—that is, not playing at all. The Expected Value of this option is exactly zero. Since the Expected Values of *all* the betting options open to a roulette player are negative, it might be suggested that the behavioral consequence, considering the option of not playing, *should* be the universal avoidance of roulette.

From the given information, however, there is no way to decide how a person *will* play roulette. This brings up the distinction between a normative theory—about what people *should* do—and a descriptive theory about what people *actually* do. Normatively, it has been shown that people shouldn't play roulette if the roulette wheel is fair and if the values of the game are accurately represented in the monetary gains and losses. Descriptively, however, many people do play roulette when given the opportunity. Why is the theory outlined unable to account for this fact? One strong possibility is that the values of the game are not adequately represented in terms of monetary gains and losses and that, in this sense, the foregoing analysis is psychologically unsophisticated.

The apparent contradiction between what people should do according to a value maximization theory and what they actually do has produced a number of attempts to improve the psychological representation of the choice situation. Modern decision theories do not assume that psychological value is a direct (linear) function of money, or that expectancies are perfectly related to objective probabilities.[2] In Chapter III, utility theory was shown to be concerned with translating monetary values into psychological values, and in Chapter II, a similar distinction was drawn between psychological probabilities, or expectancies, and the mathematical or statistical concept of probability. Both of these distinctions represent attempts to make normative decision-making models more descriptive. In fact, when psychological versions of probabilities and values are included in equations for determining the Expected Values of decision options, the resulting behavioral predictions are rather accurate under the limited conditions imposed by psychological experiments (Edwards, 1955, 1961; Galanter, 1962; Cohen & Cooper, 1961).

Any gambling game for which the odds of given outcomes are known (this includes all games of the casino type) can be evaluated in the manner illustrated above. Although this analysis may be psychologically inappropriate for the gambler, it is a good descriptive theory for the gambling

[2] "Decision theory" is currently used in two rather different senses. As used by political scientists (for example, Lane, 1963) decision theories concern the locus of decision-making powers, who the deciders are, chains of information and communication leading to and deriving from political decisions and so on. The question is: How, in a complex political-social context, do collective decisions get made, how may they be predicted, and what effects do they have. As used in psychology, economics, and statistics, "decision theory" refers to a way of analyzing the determinants for individual choices—the descriptive or normative rules pertaining to people making up their minds about what is true or what they should do. The two senses of decision—the collective and the individual—are, of course, connected.

houses. From their point of view, gambling as much as possible is perfectly rational, since the Expected Values of all casino games have a margin favoring the house.[3] Evidently, a different "psychology" operates for the casinos than for customers. In Chapter VI, this problem will be explored more thoroughly.

Can the paradigm of the standard gambling game be applied to behavioral choices that are not normally considered gambles? What about buying in the stock market? Choosing courses from a college catalog? Deciding what to do on a Saturday night? The steps required for the analysis of any decision problem may be schematized roughly as follows:

1. Identify the available choice alternatives (only those that are psychologically salient).

2. Identify the possible consequences of each alternative. The number of possible consequences is two—winning and losing—only in the simplest cases. The number of evaluatively distinct outcomes in choosing courses or going on a date should be considered as more typical.

3. Determine the expectancy associated with each distinguishable outcome. Represent this as a probability between zero and one. (Of course, the sum of the probabilities for all outcomes associated with a single choice option should equal one.)

4. Determine the psychological value or utility of each conceivable outcome. [The mathematical properties of a utility index need not be of the same order as the scale of real money (a ratio scale). However, it is difficult to make use of mathematically "weak" scales such as the ordinal. Cardinal (interval) or higher-ordered metric scales (see Siegel, 1956) are useful for making behavioral predictions.]

5. Determine the expected value for each behavior alternative (after the manner illustrated in the roulette problem).

6. Predict that the person will direct his behavior toward the outcome having the highest expected value. (There are alternatives to this kind of prediction principle. For their normative theory of games, von Neumann and Morgenstern (1947) suggested that the decider choose the outcome that would minimize the maximum possible loss. Edwards, Lindman, and Phillips (1965) have argued on both theoretical and empirical grounds that this principle is too conservative for descriptive choice theories since it assumes that the external forces influencing outcomes are always malevolent.)

The preceding list is really an elaboration of the phrase, "Behavior follows from beliefs and values." But such an analytic scheme is not

---

[3] These margins vary considerably from game to game within the casino, from over 30 percent (slot machines) to 1–2 percent (some versions of "21," or blackjack). In fact, a strategy for playing "21" has been developed by a mathematician that places the margin in favor of the player (Thorp, 1962).

always feasible. The problem is to evaluate how useful this scheme is as a way to understand individual choices and the behaviors that follow them.

CONVERGENCES IN PSYCHOLOGICAL THEORY

Until recently, this way of thinking about behavioral choices was more characteristic of economics than psychology, for it was in mathematical economics that most of the important theoretical developments have taken place. Economists have found this conception of the choice process in "economic man" useful, even though a variety of psychological problems are submerged or neglected in the analysis. Some theoretical developments within psychology, however—notably Tolman's purpose behaviorism and Lewin's dynamic field theory—led to a similar analysis of choice.

Social Learning Theory

The relation between Tolman's and Lewin's theorizing and the analytic scheme presented in the previous section is clearly illustrated by Social Learning Theory (Rotter, 1954), which in many ways represents a synthesis of Tolman's and Lewin's thinking. In Social Learning Theory, three major antecedents of behavior are considered: *expectancies, reinforcement values,* and the *psychological situation.* Expectancies are closely analogous to subjective probabilities regarding the occurrence of specified outcomes. Reinforcement values are associated with outcomes to the extent that those outcomes attract behavior. It is assumed that reinforcement values have some consistency over time, so that assessments of what is valued at one point in time may be used for predictive purposes at a later point in time.

In Social Learning Theory the analysis of behavior begins with an understanding of the psychological situation. The salient expectancies and reinforcement values are closely dependent upon the nature of the psychological situation, which presents the possible courses of behavior to a person. Once alternatives are identified, the expectancies and reinforcement values associated with those alternatives determine a quantity called "behavior potential." The assumption is then made that a person will always choose the alternative for which behavior potential is maximum.

Social learning is seen as a life-long process of acquiring and modifying expectancies about what leads to what, including generalized expectancies that may concern, for example, a person's estimation of his power to manipulate the environment. Clusters of generalized expectancies comprise what Rotter has termed "freedom of movement," a phrase that is strongly reminiscent of Lewin's field theory. Values are also modified as a result of experience and socialization. Minimum goal levels are developed through a history of success and failure at some task and are modified by different psychological situations.

The similarities between Social Learning Theory and the decision theory discussed previously are quite obvious. Cognitive abilities of the organism are represented as subjective probabilities or expectancies. Motivational characteristics are described by means of utilities or reinforcement values. The psychological situation is seen as defining realistic options for behavior. Finally, the organism is assumed to be a maximizer—always choosing the option that offers the best hope of highest payoff, maximum behavior potential, or maximum Expected Value.

An even greater convergence of psychological theories can be seen. Functionally, habits can be translated into expectancies—both representing a developed ability of the organism to execute skilled adaptive behaviors in specific situations (see Behan, 1953, and Campbell, 1963, for elaborations of this translation). Similarly, directional drives, in combination with incentives, are functionally equivalent to values in the sense in which that term has been used here. The psychological situation for the more traditional habit–drive behavior theory (of Hull or Spence, for example; see Logan, 1959) becomes a set of impinging stimuli, and these function to constrain the behavioral possibilities of the organism.

In Hull's (1952) classic system, the result of drives combined with habits in a specific stimulus setting is called *excitatory potential,* and it is conceived to be directly antecedent to behavior. Thus, this concept is in the same logistic position as behavior potential and Expected Value. Consistently, the organism is considered to execute the behavior for which excitatory potential is highest.

It is currently a matter of some indifference whether rats or men are considered to be full of habits and drives or full of expectations and utilities. The traditional cognitive and stimulus–response theories have lost their differential predictive value (see Ritchie, 1965). A number of authors have written convincing intertheory translations, thereby showing that nothing is sacred in mere terminological standards (see, for example, Feather, 1959, 1963).

Further Convergences

Other lines of contemporary theory also converge toward the proposition that behavior is a joint function of beliefs and values. The following are examples of these.

Atkinson's motivation theory   Atkinson (1957) has formulated a theory in which the motivation to achieve success is a multiplicative function of the subjective probability of success and the incentive value of success. The motivation to avoid failure is similarly a function of the subjective probability of failure and the negative incentive value of failure. Behavior results from these two motivations, which include both cognitive and affective terms.

Atkinson's model is explicitly designed to fit problems of decision making in a social context. Researchers have employed it to study some of the individual difference factors that may influence choice behavior. Reliable measures of the general tendency to "fear failure," as opposed to the tendency to "hope for success," have been developed and related to the person's characteristic level of aspiration or goal setting. Both cognitive and affective antecedents are considered to influence this process.

Attitudes as antecedents of behavior   Social attitudes provide another case in point. Since Allport's (1935) designation of attitudes as the central problem of social psychology, a considerable amount of research has been done on the subject. This is not surprising, for attitudes are generally defined as "more or less enduring dispositions to social behavior" (Allport, 1954). Thus, they have the same theoretical function as excitatory potential, behavior potential, Expected Value, and Atkinson's final motivational variable.

Attitudes are commonly considered to have both motivational and cognitive components (see Krech & Crutchfield, 1948). Some authors (for example, Fishbein & Raven, 1962) prefer to reserve "attitudes" for affective social dispositions and "beliefs" or "opinions" for cognitive social dispositions. According to this latter usage, beliefs *in the existence* of the objects of attitudes (for example, extrasensory perception or the United Nations) and *relational* beliefs about those objects (that extrasensory perception is possessed only by a few, or that the United Nations headquarters is located in New York City) are to be distinguished from attitudes about those beliefs. Examples of attitudes are that extrasensory perception is a desirable human capability and that the United Nations ought to be moved out of New York.

Note the similarity between the following quotation regarding attitudes and the previously cited formulations of behavior in terms of decision theory:

> An individual's attitudes toward any object is a function of (1) the strength of his beliefs about the object and (2) the evaluative aspect of those beliefs. Algebraically, it may be predicted that an individual's attitude toward any object is equal to the sum of the product of beliefs and their respective evaluations over all aspects of the object. (Fishbein, 1965, p. 117)

A great amount of research in social psychology has focused on attitudes as dependent variables. Persuasion and propaganda are seen as processes of attitude change (Hovland, Janis, & Kelley, 1953). The "authoritarian personality" is characterized by a set of rigid attitudes (Adorno *et al.*, 1950). Attitudes are considered subject to the pressures of social conformity, and also to pressures toward consistency with other attitudes held (Zajonc, 1960).

In most research on attitudes, the questionnaire has replaced direct behavioral observation. This is reasonable if we assume that attitudes are, in fact, tendencies to action. In stating an attitude, a person is supposed to be telling the psychologist how he *would* respond to some set of hypothetical circumstances. Unfortunately, few studies critically explore the relation between stated social attitudes and actual social behavior.[4] Reference has already been made to the discrepancy between expressions of racial tolerance and actual discriminatory behavior such as refusal to rent or to employ members of minority groups. The demands imposed by verbal (questionnaire) statements are different from the demands imposed by real decisions involving minority group members. Stating an attitude on a questionnaire is not the same behavior as a full scale enactment of the phrase, "I would rent property to blacks as readily as to whites." Thus, the beliefs and values that apply to the statement of an attitude are quite different from the beliefs and values that apply to enacting that attitude.

Social role theory   Two of the major concepts in role theory—role expectations and norms—are also translations of beliefs and values. In role theory (Sarbin, 1954; Sarbin & Allen, 1968), the basic behavioral proposition is that behavior results from the interaction between a person and a role associated with a position (status) in the social structure. Thus, an elected official brings certain personal characteristics to his position, which itself carries, by social convention or tradition, certain expectations about how a person in that position is supposed to act.

Both the occupant of a status and those around him have expectations about performances that are proper for his role. These expectations are implicit directions concerning how the role should be performed. A major determinant of effectiveness in role enactment is the agreement of the person and his audience on these expectations—that is, how well a person "knows his part."

Every role also carries a set of invoked social norms and socially implemented evaluations of the adequacy of performance. Thus, norms of politeness are invoked for the role of dinner guest, and evaluations are made in terms of behavioral consistency with the rules about politeness in this particular setting. To pose another example, it is generally the

---

[4] Those studies that have explored the relation between expressed attitude and actual behavior have generally demonstrated an inconsistency in these two modes of expression. For example, LaPiere's (1934) classic study showed that face to face behavior between members of minority groups and landlords differed considerably from the pious liberality expressed in attitude questionnaires.

norm that professors wear neckties to class, and those who do not are evaluated as eccentric. By contrast, students in most parts of the United States are not expected to wear neckties to class; in some places they may even be ridiculed for doing so, as a form of negative social evaluation. Various norms are also characterized by a "range of tolerance" (see Jackson, 1965) within which deviations are tolerated or positively rewarded. Of course, the major determinant of the size of this range is the referent social group (or audience), who in effect decide how much deviance will be tolerated before a person is considered so "far out" that he requires negative sanctioning.

The dominant values, or norms, of a society may be found by examining its sanctioning rules. Norms of propriety demand that individuals respect certain rights of others, and "troublemakers" or "public nuisances" are often jailed—in a prison or a mental hospital. That norms change is evidenced by changes in the sanctioning rules and inconsistencies in their application. Possession of alcohol is not now a crime in the United States, but it was in the 1920s. Possession of marijuana is now a crime in the United States, but there are great differences in the willingness of various subsectors of our society to enforce this social norm with appropriate sanctions. Thus, many things appear to be right or wrong by social convention, quite independently of their survival value, their drive-satisfying characteristics, their capacity to reduce tissue needs, or their correspondence with man's basic "instincts."

Most behavior takes place in a social context, and role theory—drawn by analogy from the drama—aims at providing an account of such behavior. Each man is seen as behaving in a highly differentiated social structure—a structure that imparts to the occupant of each position both knowledge of the part (beliefs) and evaluations of the adequacy of performances (values). Role theory is avowedly interactional, always including personal *and* ecological characteristics as determinants of the saliency of a particular set of beliefs and values. Babbitt at an out-of-town convention is the same man as church-going Babbitt at home. But the change of physical setting and relevant audience brings such a shift in salient beliefs and values that radically different behaviors are demonstrated in the two settings.

Recapitulation   The grouping of this list of theories—decision theory, Social Learning Theory, S–R theory, attitude theory, Atkinson's motivational theory, the role theory—does not imply that all really say the same thing when superficial differences are eliminated. Certainly, the types of psychological problems to which these various theories are congenial and the precision with which they are stated are quite different.

However, the commonality among these approaches encourages the abstraction of beliefs and values as dominant antecedents to behavior.

Each theory implies that man is both a knowing and a wanting creature. Each theory implies that the combination of these dispositions with inputs from the environment determines behavior. The relation between social attitudes and behaviors remains ill defined. Role theory is enormously flexible in that it does not specify the content of norms and expectations that determine social behavior. But the rest of the theories mentioned in this section also agree that man is a maximizing creature—always operating on the central principle of collective bargaining: the desire for MORE.

Not long ago the view of motives held by psychologists—based on the principle of tension reduction—and the view of utility held by economists—based on the principle of inexhaustible greed—led to very different images of the fulfilled man. The psychologist's man was either comatose or dead, and the economist's man resembled Scrooge McDuck, Walt Disney's insatiable billionaire. This divergence ended when psychology accepted the motives for exploration, competence, and curiosity, and when behavioral decision theories developed as a bridge between economics and psychology. Excepting attitude theory and role theory from consideration, the composite man that emerges from psychological theory is striving, purposive, and calculating. The prototype of modern psychological man is neither dead nor excessively rich. Instead, he is knowledgeable, well traveled, competent, skillful, only "comfortably" wealthy, and cool-headed. Perhaps the movie spy is the ultimate model of man deduced from this group of contemporary psychological theories.

DIFFICULTIES

Unfortunately, experimental evidence for the ecological validity of descriptive decision theories is weak. Even if these theories do not predict the behavior of monks or avant-garde artists, they should be expected to account for the behavior of man in the marketplace. Yet a psychologist specializing in economic behavior notes that

> Experimental studies of the decision-making process have been intended primarily to investigate choice behavior under certain artificially restricted conditions (e.g. gambling situations in which complete or fairly complete information was given about chances or risks). It has not yet been shown that an experimental clarification of postulates of economic theory about rational behavior has direct relevance to the understanding of how businessmen and consumers actually behave. (Katona, 1963, p. 672)

Other writers who have reviewed the experimental literature on decision and choice behavior have arrived at similar conclusions (Edwards, 1961; Simon, 1963). At present, psychology has not developed any widely acceptable way of formulating the relationship between beliefs and values (as antecedents) and behavior (as a consequence or dependent variable). some of the major problems in relating beliefs and values to behavior are considered below.

Multidimensional Utility: The Comparability of Values

In Chapter III the problem of exchange rates, or the translatability of values was mentioned. Economists often assume that a general function relates one kind of value, such as physical comfort, to another kind, such as money. But most complex decisions, such as where to spend a vacation, involve an array of apparently separate values—expense, opportunity for recreation, travel time, climate, and the opinions of other people, for example. But ultimately a person must choose one site over all the others, or stay home. Therefore, he must effectively decide whether a certain amount of extra sunshine is worth x dollars of additional expense.

The problem for psychological theory is not the existence of different kinds of value (multiple dimensions of value). Nor does there seem to be much question, on the theoretical level, that somehow individuals form a single aggregate preference for an option involving many different kinds of value. For example, many people act as if the pleasure of smoking cigarettes is greater than the combination of increased danger to health, the price of cigarettes, stained teeth, and perhaps occasional social disapproval. The problem for psychological theory is to demonstrate that the conversion of multiple values into a single preference is an *orderly* process.

The basic issue is the *consistency* of preference behavior, both within the same person over a period of time and among different individuals. One of the assumptions involved in utility scaling is that preferences are *transitive;* that is, if a person prefers chocolate ice cream to strawberry ice cream, and strawberry to vanilla, he ought to prefer chocolate to vanilla. The requirement for transitivity of choice is that preference hierarchies remain consistently ordered over time. Unfortunately, evidence is ample that preference hierarchies are not perfectly constant over time and that many people express preferences in an intransitive fashion. The writer once obtained supervisory evaluations of employees in an insurance company and found that about 20 percent of the supervisors made statements of the following kind: Tom Jones is a better worker than Bill Logan; Bill Logan is a better worker than Bruce Smith; Bruce Smith is a better worker than Tom Jones. Of course it may be that when Jones and Logan were compared, the supervisor was thinking of piece-work output, and when Logan and Smith were compared, he was thinking of compatibility with other workers as the evaluative criterion. Thus, failure to reduce multiple value dimensions to a common utility scale may account for shifting preference hierarchies and intransitive choices.

Commodity prices evidently represent somebody's judgment about the aggregate value of the multiple advantages acquired from a new purchase, such as a car or television set. But agreement among individuals on the justice of pricing conventions is much less than the degree of consistency in one person's values. It may be comforting for decision theory to cite the maxim, "Everything has its price," but it is discomforting to note the fragility of social agreements about what those prices should be.

The Equivocal Relation of Decision to Behavior

Decisions and behaviors are not coterminous; decisions do not automatically produce actions. Perhaps the confusion between these phenomena derives from the study of choice processes in the rat, in which the physical pursuit of some alternative is the only index of choice. But in man, the distinction between deciding upon a course of action and consummating that decision is more obvious. "To cease smoking," Mark Twain remarked, "is the easiest thing I ever did . . . I've done it a thousand times."

Clearly, psychology must include reference to ability factors, such as intelligence, coordination, and perceptual-motor skills, in any full accounting of behavior. This must be recognized as a limitation of any psychology based upon beliefs and values. We may account for a person's pretended actions, but the outcomes of those actions are not determined by beliefs and values—usually. Beliefs and values are psychological antecedents to a decision. After the decision is made, it is presumed that the conflicts among competing options will have little effect on the outcome of the behavior, which is a problem outside the scope of beliefs and values.

Is Man a Maximizer? If So, of What?

Simon (1963) has noted that "the assumptions of economic theory that have been most challenged are its motivational assumptions—particularly the consistency of preferences of humans and their exclusive preoccupation with monetary rewards" (p. 694). The first of these challenges has been taken up in the section on multidimensional utilities. The problem of monetary reward is even more serious for predictive choice theories, for it removes the assumption that allows behavioral predictions to be drawn from situations that are completely defined in terms of expectancies and utilities. Simon (1956) has suggested as an alternative that man, and men acting together in corporations, do not behave in a way that maximizes conventional profit, but more characteristically live according to what he has called a "satisficing" regime.

Without much reflection we see that it is prejudicial and arbitrary to identify money making with rationality. Maximization of money is certainly not necessary to survival under most circumstances, and it may actually be unfavorable to survival, as attested by the notorious ulcer problems of competitive businessmen. The alternative presented by Simon is a behavior model in which the organism moves from one "satisficing node" (like a refueling station) to the next in its behavioral field at quite a leisurely pace. The organism moves on only when the level of resources required for its meandering existence is depleted. It does not try to stuff itself or to get rich.

Preoccupation with the pursuit of profit and with the accumulation of capital seems to be especially strong in some regions, such as northern Europe and the United States, and quite diminished in others, such as Latin America and the Polynesian Islands (see McCelland, 1961). Regardless of the truth of Max Weber's well-known thesis that this difference is attributable to the "Protestant ethic" in Europe and the United States, the difference itself remains an embarrassment to the principle of maximization.

In most psychological experiments on decision and choice, subjects are *instructed* to maximize their gain. For example, Edwards (1955) reports that "each S was told that his purpose in the experiment was to make as much money as possible" (p. 203). Galanter (1962) also told his subjects that "the idea is to make as much money as possible" (p. 217). In nongambling choice experiments, subjects are characteristically told to try to maximize the number of correct predictions of events. If nothing else, these instructions are testimony to the possibility that subjects might perversely do something other than maximize.

Simon (1956) has argued that many business firms do not operate in such a way as to maximize profit, and that they choose this course knowingly and rationally. Although public relations offices serve the major function of drumming the product, they also help create a corporate image that offers nonprofit satisfaction to the owners and the public.

This has important implications for behavior theory. In Social Learning Theory, for example, we must ask why a person is always considered to choose the alternative for which behavior potential is maximum. If the reply is that the choice itself is evidence for the highest quantity of behavior potential among a set of options, then the definition of behavior potential is circular and vacuous. Theorists are then driven toward an "out" that has frequently been taken in the history of psychology—the invention of dispositions to go with the actions they are to explain.

Values as redescriptions of behavior   The option for an economist who is trying to understand why firms may not maximize profits is to broaden the definition of "profit." Good repute, satisfaction with the high quality of production, and sentiments connected with money-losing operations (such as San Francisco's cable cars) may be seen as example of this more extended conception of profit.

Essentially the same solution was adopted by psychologists when they realized that not all of man's behavior could be accounted for in terms of a few basic biological drives, such as hunger, thirst, and sex. They began to recognize other drives or motives that corresponded to large categories of apparently irreducible behavior, such as exploration, curiosity, or creativity. This solution, of course, may amount to exactly the same kind of circularity noted in the preceding section. Thus, altruistic behavior may be attributed to a person's motive to give succorance, and avarice may be attributed to the hoarding instinct. Hitler organized mass extermination campaigns because of his sadism, and Schweitzer tried to save a colony of lepers because of his love of man.

While these designations in no way explain the behaviors they describe, they are good shorthand descriptions of that behavior. Moreover, the norms of consistency offer some hope that they may have predictive use. If values are named in this redescriptive way, then the question of their stability is an empirical matter.

Clearly, the maximization assumption is gratuitous unless what is being maximized is specified ahead of time. This is not a simple matter, for if persons are endowed with the potential for *opposing* motives—such as life and death—then it is impossible that both can be maximized at once. At the same time, it is inevitable that any particular action will correspond to one value or the other.

What happens if a universal maximization assumption is rejected? How might beliefs and values then be related to behavior? This possibility is explored in the next section.

A SYNTHETIC MODEL: SOCIAL ROLES AS THE CONTEXT OF CHOICE

As customarily discussed (Sarbin, 1954; Sarbin & Allen, 1968), role theory contains no clear and explicit parallel to the maximization assumption that has just been set forth. How cognitive and motivational dispositions of the person are translated into behavior in specific circumstances has yet to be specified. However, role theory makes the assumption that man maximizes his gain unnecessary, and instead allocates this assumption to a class of special rules that may be applied to the occupants of social positions.

The thesis in this section is that the operation of beliefs and values must be viewed in the context of ongoing social behavior, and that role theory provides the appropriate terms for the analysis of social behavior. In Chapter I we saw that beliefs and values enter only into analyses of behaviors that are "rule following" rather than "caused." Similarly, role theory is concerned only with this kind of behavior. The fundamental assumption adopted by role theory is that "man is a rule-following animal" (Peters, 1958). Like the conventional rules for games such as Monopoly or bridge all rules are comprised—psychologically—of beliefs and values. In a recent article, Allen (1968) states this relationship between rules and roles quite well:

> All societies conventionalize behavior; even in the case of biologically based behavior such as food seeking and sexual activity, expression is governed by an elaborate set of rules which differs across cultures. Rules also govern the behavior of persons having specific statuses in society —such as husband or wife, teacher or student, host or guest. Rules for a particular social position are role-expectations which define how the occupant of the position ought to behave. Such role-expectations exist for each social position within a society and define the appropriate behavior for an occupant of the position. We can say . . . that man is a rule-following animal, and further that roles constitute the rules for behaving appropriately in accord with one's social position. (p. 202–203)

Role theory contains no statements about the content of rules or about what rules *should* be. Thus, role theory is descriptive rather than normative. Indeed, the task for psychological analysis from the perspective of role theory is to discover the content of the rules that apply to a segment of behavior. Role theorists share with all psychologists the assumption that behavior is systematic and regular, and thus, analyzable. But role theorists are perhaps unique in their insistence that systematic regularities in behavior can be discovered only by attention to social conditions and conventions. The theory contains no universal specifications of social conventions, but is "filled" in any applied case by reference to the particular set of beliefs and values carried by the target person, group, or culture.

A Model in Six Stages[5]

The line between purposive, rule-following behavior and other forms of behavior is not absolute. In order to define more clearly the kinds of behaviors that are subject to analysis in terms of beliefs and values, we must have a set of behavior paradigms, defined in terms of the complex-

---

[5] It is something of a current fad to talk of models where previously the term "theory" might have been used. While formal distinctions between theories and models might be offered (see Chapanis, 1961), the latter term is preferred here because it has the connotation of a self-conscious analogy—as a suggestion of a useful way of looking at things rather than a guess as to how things "really are."

ity of psychological processes and in terms of specifically appropriate analytic categories.

Six distinct levels of complexity in the relation of an object (or organism) to its ecology may be described as six distinct paradigms for behavior:

Stage 1.   Consider an undifferentiated object in an undifferentiated field. A billiard ball resting on a table will do for an example. In a sense, this is a completely degenerate behavioral model, for nothing is happening. The psychological condition of the subject—the billiard ball—is one of zero activation. No living person fits this paradigm.

Stage 2.   Consider an undifferentiated object in an undifferentiated but *dynamic* field. A billiard ball on a table will again serve as an example, but the table must be tilted. (Another example would be a steel ball that is placed on a plane surface and attracted in one direction by a magnet.) In this case, something is happening, but to describe it is a problem for physical mechanics rather than psychology. The psychological condition of the subject is one of completely undifferentiated and "unintelligent" activation—somewhat below the level of the vegetable. Human beings in protracted comas may fit this paradigm, for their activity over time is constant and it is dependent upon the "energy" supplied from external sources.

Stage 3.   The next degree of complexity may be represented by a differentiated object in a differentiated dynamic field. An imperfect pinball rolling through the mazes and pathways of the machine provides a physical example. Again, physics is the discipline best suited to examine this type of behavior. Things are happening in this case, and the course of events changes abruptly over time, always as a function of the interaction of the object and its contacted environment. A psychological example would be a person convulsed with panic who tries to escape from a burning building, as in the famous Coconut Grove or Hartford circus fires. Behavior fitting this paradigm is caused rather than reasoned, and it cannot be analyzed appropriately in terms of role theory or beliefs and values.

Stage 4.   An increasing degree of complexity is introduced if we maintain all of the features of the previous stages and add the ability of an object to sense and *anticipate* external occurrences. The differentiated object in the differentiated field must now be equipped with advanced sensing and motoric devices. An object may be given these properties by appropriate electronic gadgetry, such as light-sensitive photo cells, thermocouplings, and feedback circuits. A guided missile satisfies the requirements of this stage, as do a rat wandering through a maze and a person walking in a park. Clearly, the behavior of the last two examples is of psychological interest. The rat and the human ordinarily avoid barriers on such ventures; perceptual mechanisms and motoric skills make such control possible. An advanced phase of this stage includes the addition of reprogramming or "learning" devices to the subject. This has been accomplished mechanically in a machine that automatically eliminates for itself the possibility of repeating the last action before any failure (using the principle of negative reinforcement) (Block, 1965).

Stage 5. Still further complication is introduced by endowing the subject (or the behaving mechanism) with unique evaluative capacities. The subject can now anticipate events and the consequences of actions, as in Stage 4, but has the further capacity to make individual value judgments about alternative goals. Some chess-playing machines evaluate the available playing options and make choices that implement their preferences. Other computing machines solve problems intelligently and rather unpredictably (Newell, Simon, & Shaw, 1958). Such machines utilize both anticipatory and evaluative mechanisms.

Obviously much human and animal behavior fits this paradigm. The behavior of a football quarterback provides a good example. The game has an overall objective (values are defined) and a variety of play possibilities; the outcome of any play is jointly determined by subject (quarterback) and by ecological factors (everyone else on both teams, plus the weather and terrain).

Decision theories are appropriate for the analysis of behaviors at this level, and most of the experiments on choice, decision, and laboratory gambling behavior are consistent with this paradigm. Frequently, the principle of maximization of utility gives good predictive results, especially if instructions to follow it are given.

Stage 6. Does man possess basic capacities beyond those implied in Stage 5? Although most people like to think that man is superior to animals or machines there are provocative arguments that machines could be built to simulate human behavior convincingly (see Turing, 1963, for example). However, it is generally difficult to establish a negative affirmation, and it is twice as difficult to prove the negation of the superior uniqueness of man. Man is not clever enough to prove that he is no more clever than the rest of the natural world.

This conundrum conveys a human characteristic that indeed passes beyond the Stage 5 paradigm—namely, the capacity for self-reference,[6] with accompanying developments in symbolic and abstractive abilities.

---

[6] Bronowski (1966) states that the self-reference capacities of man logically preclude the possibility of developing a complete and systematic description of the determination of human events. "It follows from my view that the unwritten aim that the physical sciences have set themselves since Isaac Newton's time cannot be attained. The laws of nature cannot be formulated as an axiomatic, deductive, formal and unambiguous system which is also complete. And if at any stage in scientific discovery the laws of nature did seem to make a complete system, then we should have to conclude that we have not got them right. . . . There is no perfect description conceivable, even in the abstract, in the form of an axiomatic

Man has values about his values—for example, that it is not right to take pleasure in aggression—and beliefs about his beliefs—for example, that all beliefs are probabilistic. Man is the builder of abstract systems, the dweller in mythic structures, the creator and appreciator of fictions about himself and his world. Stage 6 is an appropriate paradigm for the philosopher,[7] the cosmologist, the scientist, and the actor. To the extent that Everyman corresponds with the practitioners of these professions, Stage 6 must be invoked as an appropriate level of discussion for Everyman's behavior.

A hallmark of Stage 6 behavior is abstractive flexibility—the capacity to move from level to level in thinking and behavior. Man can live vicariously in many worlds, and he can respond vicariously to persons and groups that do not physically impinge upon the sensorium. From Stage 6 a man descends into the behavioral settings provided by lower stages—most importantly, Stage 5. While an actor is speaking his lines, he is a subject in the Stage 5 paradigm, as is any person who has a high temporary involvement in one of his roles (such as parent, club member, or volleyball player). Behavior in these roles is rule following, and the beliefs and values that comprise those rules must be stated explicitly in order that the behavior be understood. But an actor is more than an active player—he is a person, with a repertoire both in and out of the theatre. As the self-conscious developer of new parts, as one who reflects on how things *should* be, as the confused and doubting, wondering man, he is back at Stage 6. At Stage 6, man is not as much the object of psychologies as he is the maker of them.

Roles as the Premises for Decision and Action

Simon (1963) has stated a definition of social roles that helps to clarify the sense of the foregoing discussion:

A role . . . is a social prescription of some, but not all, of the premises that enter into an individual's choices of behaviors. Any particular concrete behavior is the result of a large number of premises, only some of which are prescribed by the role. In addition to role premises, there are premises about the state of the environment based directly on perception, premises representing beliefs and knowledge, and idiosyncratic premises that characterize the personality. (p. 713)

---

and deductive system" (p. 5). Further, Bronowski notes the special relevance of these limitations to the social and psychological sciences, where, of course, any stated laws of behavior must apply to the behavior of those stating the laws. "They [psychology, and so forth] are limited, more severely and more constantly than the natural sciences, by the self-reference that underlies them everywhere" (p. 10).
[7] "That self-knowledge is the highest aim of philosophical inquiry appears to be generally acknowledged." (Cassirer, 1954, p. 15)

(The latter qualifications correspond to the conventional statements in role theory that behavior results from characteristics of the *self* and the *ecology* as well as from the role itself.[8])

The behavior of subjects in psychological experiments is a good example of the way in which roles furnish premises. In terms of the previous six-stage model, a subject is at the Stage 6 level before his appearance at the laboratory; that is, he is a reflective human being. But when he enters the laboratory, he assumes the role of experimental subject (Stage 5), and he behaves according to the rules implied in that role.

The arriving subject is initially passive, receptive, and relatively uncommunicative. It is the role of the experimenter to give "Instructions" to the subject, so that he knows what is expected of him. The subject typically displays a "problem-solving set"—he wants to know what the experiment is all about. While he often distrusts the truth of the explanation, he knows that he is not supposed to question overtly the "cover story." In addition, he usually holds other evaluative premises: The subject wants to make the experiment succeed, but he knows he should be honest and avoid "confusing" the experiment by conspicuously manipulating his responses. The subject typically wants to maintain his self-image as an honest person, while at the same time making a contribution to science by participating in a successful experiment.[9]

Thus, both the explicit and the implicit instructions to an arriving subject tell him what he is supposed to attempt (maximize his winnings in gambling; learn nonsense syllables as rapidly as possible; solve a puzzle; state his "true" attitudes toward minority groups, and so on). These defined goals, in addition to the previously mentioned general reasons of subjects for participating in experiments, comprise the values that operate in this setting.

Belief, or expectations, are also provided by instructions. For example, subjects are shown what happens if a button is pressed; how a memory drum operates; how they can request further information and so on.

Given these cognitive and motivational premises, the experiment

---

[8] Sarbin *et al.* (1960) have developed a detailed cognitive theory to account for the process of combining premises, carried by both self and role, with perceptual rules (which Sarbin *et al.* call "instantiations") for the formation of novel conclusions. In particular, the role of the clinical psychologist is examined in this work. The values of the clinical psychologist are implicit in his role, and his beliefs are taken from courses, textbooks, and the informal accumulation of experiences. In the present context Sarbin *et al.* (1960) have provided a very good explication of the rules that apply to the cognitive behavior of the clinical diagnostician.

[9] Implicit premises in a psychological experiment often go unrecognized by the experimenter. Thus, the presence of medical instruments and the assurance that no danger is involved in the experiment often produces the expectation that the experiment *might be* dangerous. Moreover, the conventional practice of pre-testing and post-testing subjects around an intervening treatment produces the implicit demand for change in performance on the tests. See Orne and Scheibe (1964) for an experiment illustrating these principles.

proceeds quite predictably, and psychologist can be effective at providing good and convincing analyses of the details of laboratory behavior. But when instructions are vague, ambiguous, or patently false, the experiment inevitably runs into trouble—for this amounts to uncertainty about the nature of the role, and the resultant behavior is far too variable to be useful.

Good experimenters are careful to instruct their subjects thoroughly, so that interpretable results can be obtained. An example is provided by Duncker's (1945) research on problem solving. Duncker defined a problem as a situation in which a person wants a given solution, but does not know how to arrive at that solution. His subjects were instructed to attempt the problems which Duncker provided, and they adopted as their goals the legitimate attainment of the specified solutions.

In the classic x-ray problem, the subject tries to formulate a satisfactory method of destroying an inoperable stomach tumor by means of irradiation, without destroying surrounding tissue. If the subject does not adopt this fictional goal, his subsequent behavior is unpredictable and nonsensical for the purposes of the experiment. With the adoption of this goal, however, the subject proceeds to formulate (aloud, as per instruction) partial solutions to the problem, utilizing both knowledge (beliefs) that he brings with him (for example, that rays travel in straight lines) and knowledge provided by the experimenter (for example, that more than one source of radiation is permitted). Given these premises, the behavior of the subject is quite orderly, consisting of a series of problem reformulations occurring with some predictable order and emphasis. From his results, Duncker was able to formulate a theoretical description of problem solving that has served succeeding generations of psychologists. A model of problem solving very similar to the one proposed by Duncker was as explicitly constructed that a simulating program written for a computer produced results very like those produced by living (Stage 5) subjects (Newell & Simon, 1963). Psychology has come a long way toward understanding problem solving because of these efforts, but it is only problem solving of this specific kind—conducted under these kinds of instructions and constraints—that is elucidated. Other types of problems may bring different beliefs and values into play.

The behavior of a businessman, for example, which might appear paradoxical from the standpoint of the assumption of profit maximization, is not paradoxical from the present point of view. Maximization of profit is but *one* operating premise that may apply to certain business positions, and there are many other such evaluative premises. The values relevant to the manager of a traditional British producer of fine woolens differ appreciably from the values imposed on the manager of a drive-in restaurant in a highly competitive region. Profit maximization, it is likely, would be a much more salient demand for the latter businessman.

Similarly, the behavior of the tourist passing through Las Vegas is not constrained by the same role expectations that apply to casino operators. The tourist is on vacation, having fun, he is carefree and perhaps a little silly with money. Casino operators, on the other hand, are seriously concerned with earning money and running a business. Because these two roles perfectly complement each other, the system continues to function smoothly.

Whether one looks upon roles as composed of rules, expectations, or premises is largely a matter of semantic preference, for all three terms are appropriately descriptive. When a subject enters a new situation, a set of effective guides for behavior in that situation are formulated; these guides are a product of the beliefs and values that a person brings with him, as well as a result of the cognitive and motivational information offered in the situation. We can easily see the operation of these rules in conventional settings, such as cricket matches and baseball games, even though the rules themselves may be enormously complex. But other settings for which no written rulebooks exist—elevators, classrooms, parked cars, discotheques, and battle fields—follow the same principles. Operative beliefs and values emerge from the combination of persons with ecological settings, and through an explication of these beliefs and values some understanding of a person's behavior in that setting may be gained.

SUMMARY

We can understand without difficulty how beliefs influence behavior when values are constant (the quest for a missing object) and how values may influence behavior when beliefs are constant (selecting among equally available outcomes). But when both beliefs and values vary freely (as in gambling games), the problem is somewhat more complicated. A conventional procedure exists, generic to a set of behavior theories in psychology and economics that translate known expectancies and utilities into predictions of behavior. Generally, these theories make an assumption that behavior is an attempt to maximize something. In economic theory, utility (or profit) is maximized; in psychological theory, motive or need satisfaction is maximized.

Difficulties arise when these principles are generalized to relate beliefs and values with behavior, especially if one is scrupulous about avoiding the endless creation of ad hoc motives to explain a given unit of behavior. Among the difficulties are (a) the lack of identity between a decision and the execution of behavior; (b) the weak evidence for the consistency of human preferences over time and situations; and (c) the evidence that many individuals and businesses do not maximize an ordinary sort of profit.

A schematization of behavior through increasingly complex levels or "stages" reveals that certain kinds of analysis are appropriate for certain levels of complexity, and other kinds of analysis for other levels. The penultimate level of complexity (Stage 5) is one in which belief-value analyses are quite appropriate; here conventional decision theories may apply, but the *content* of operative beliefs and values must be specified. Roles may be looked upon as social conventions providing operational premises in specific circumstances. Other premises for behavior are carried in the person (self) or are applied through perceptual inputs. The task of psychological analysis, from this perspective, is to develop a good description of the content of resultant behavior rules in some behavioral setting.

The more complex behavioral paradigm (Stage 6) is characterized by a self-reflective person, capable of thinking and "living" flexibly at various levels of abstraction. It is helpful to view persons over their life span as "dwelling in" this stage during those periods in which role expectations are relatively undefined—that is, when the person is between Stage 5 performances. Theory at the Stage 6 level does not specify the nature and content of beliefs and values or social roles. But when the situation becomes defined for a person—such as a subject in a psychological experiment or a business manager being given his operating instructions—behavior becomes conventionalized according to the joint characteristics of the person and the role. The maximization assumption may be an appropriate analytic assumption (probably it often is), but only if the behaving person has been told or tells himself to be a maximizer.

The rules for the translation of beliefs and values into behavior vary for a person from setting to setting, and role theory must be invoked for possibility. The synthesis of role theory and a theory of choice permits the tracing of a much wider range or consistency and order in behavior than is possible with either theory employed singly.

V

Transformations in Beliefs and Values: Research Issues

Skepticism, while logically impeccable, is psychologically impossible.   **Bertrand Russell**

FROM SEVERAL PERSPECTIVES, we have concluded that it is incorrect to view beliefs and values as constant personal entities. When a person enters a behavioral setting, operative beliefs and values emerge which depend upon both personal dispositions and the social (public) definition of that setting. The emphasis on this interaction does not, however, obscure the fact that individuals differ strongly in what they are disposed to believe and in what they are disposed to value. Witnesses of a crime, for example, are known to differ in their reports of the "facts," customers at an auction vary in their dispositions to bid on the objects offered for sale, and teachers will readily attest to motivational and cognitive differences among students.

The existence of these differences among individuals leads to a consideration of developmental issues. How do personal dispositions to believe and to value change over time? What are the developmental origins of beliefs and values? Can values act as antecedents to beliefs, and beliefs as antecedents to values? If so, under what conditions does each occur?

The developmental issues suggest another set of research questions, for individuals differ not only in what they believe and value, but also in the way in which they use new experience to modify their behavioral dispositions. Dogmatism, rigidity, open-mindedness, and rationality are terms commonly used to describe how a person's beliefs and values are affected or unaffected by new information and experiences. Do these terms

86

represent observable psychological processes? If so, what are the origins and effects of these processes?

Considerable research relevant to these issues has accumulated, and we will invoke this literature when it is pertinent. But the more inclusive objective is to display and clarify some of the problems that serve as challenges for future research.

CHANGES OF MIND

We will find it useful to refer here to the distinction drawn in Chapter II between the distal ecology (the external world of occurrence) and the cognitive representation of that ecology (the product of past experience and the substrate of operative beliefs). In view of this, the difference between a rat experienced in a maze and a naive rat is that the experienced rat has formed some functional representation of the maze. In the task of analyzing behavior, a crucial difference between an experienced clinical psychologist and the layman is that the clinical psychologist has learned a highly specialized set of rules ("modular organization," in the terms of Sarbin, Taft, & Bailey, 1960), which he uses as the basis for diagnosis and prognosis. According to Hebb (1949), experience produces in the perceiving organism an organization of neural "cell assemblies," which function as perceptual expectancies, permitting the rapid and efficient identification of familiar external occurrences. The difference in reference problems for these theories accounts for differences in terminology. In all cases, however, the central idea is that organisms are capable of accumulating an informational structure from which it is possible to draw expectancies as occasion demands. In the idiom of the present discussion, it is beliefs that are drawn on demand from this implicit informational structure.

Genetic Differences

In contemporary psychology it is readily agreed that differences in the adaptive possibilities of various species are related to inherent capacities for the formation of informational structures. Human beings are capable of learning more complex materials than are monkeys, monkeys can solve problems that baffle rats, and rats are cognitively superior to many more primitive organisms (worms, starfish, and salamanders, for example). Within a single species, however, differences in inherent cognitive capacities have been the subject of more dispute, and the current questions concern the details and causes of genetic differences within a species. Strains of "bright" and "dull" rats have been developed, and evidence from studies of human twins reared together and reared apart is consistent with the conclusion that cognitive capacities are at least partly determined by genetic factors (see Thompson, 1967; McClearn & Rodgers, 1961; Dobzhansky, 1962).

Students of psychological linguistics have recently offered impressive arguments for the existence in human beings of an inherited, or "preprogrammed," information-processing structure (see Miller, 1962). Rules for the production and understanding of complex sentences are thought to be part of the "nature of the beast." The ability to use words is not a product of simple S–R conditioning based upon associative repetition, but it is a combination of a characteristic "pre-wiring" of the human central nervous system and the linguistic and grammatical conventions to which a person is exposed during his development. Moreover, there is strong presumptive evidence for "critical periods"[1] in the development of language. Individuals growing up in verbally impoverished environments never seem to acquire the ability of peers who spend their infancy and childhood amid rich verbal stimulation (see Hunt, 1961).

Although a discussion of psycholinguistics is inappropriate here, we must recognize the enormous cognitive advantage that man's symbolic language abilities impart to him. Man acquires information with much more flexibility than would be possible if the capacity for symbolic language were absent. Hence, any discussion about how man changes his mind—how he acquires or modifies beliefs—must take as a presupposition the existence of a flexible and potentially superefficient information-processing system.

Whereas genetic factors determine the existence of such capacities in man, the development of a cognitive structure with specific content is due to environmental inputs. Given two organisms with similar natural heredity, differences in their ability to "think" and to "solve problems" must be traced to differences in postnatal experiences.

A Normative Model for Mind-changing

In view of the theory developed earlier that beliefs may be described as probabilistic (uncertain), the problem of changing beliefs becomes one

---

[1] The concept of "critical periods" was developed by ethologists (see Cofer & Apley, 1964) to account for certain observations associated with "imprinting" in birds. If a young duckling is exposed, during a certain period after hatching, to a target object with certain defined characteristics (size, color, mobility, and so forth), it will develop a lasting attraction for that object, or "imprint" to it. Beyond a certain period after hatching (the exact limits vary from species to species and form a subject for experimental dispute), the occurrence of target objects in the field of the young bird have no effect. This phenomenon has been related, at least analogically, to the dependence of human infants upon certain kinds of stimulation during certain periods of development. It is known that human infants reared in very dull and uniform stimulus environments show inferior cognitive performance at a later period and seem irreversibly handicapped (see Hunt, 1961).

of changing the probabilities associated with uncertain propositions. Before Magellan, for example, it was considered improbable that a man could sail around the world; when the feat had been accomplished, this evidence increased the expectation that future voyages would be successful. Lindbergh's transatlantic flight seemed very risky to many, but today hundreds of persons board planes daily for a similar flight, with virtual certainty that they will arrive safely.

We can conclude, then, that new information about possible events alters beliefs by increasing or decreasing their likelihood. For scientists performing experiments, a critical question concerns just what impact new information should have upon preexisting beliefs. Experiments are costly, and most scientists are required to "maximize" in the sense of producing the greatest amount of "truth" for the least cost in dollars. How many experiments will be necessary to prove that new information is conclusive? How much evidence on the toxic properties of a novel drug is needed before there is sufficient certainty of its safety for general consumption? How much evidence for the reality of ESP should psychic researchers produce for their basic conclusions to be accepted by the scientific community?

This problem may be seen more clearly in an experimental procedure developed by Edwards, Lindman, and Phillips (1965). Two book bags containing mixtures of red and blue poker chips were used. In one bag there was a majority (perhaps 70 percent) of red chips, and in the other an equal majority of blue chips. A subject was allowed to sample chips, one at a time, from one of the bags; he was then asked to estimate the likelihood that the bag being sampled contained a majority of red (or blue) chips. If only one chip was sampled, the subject could have concluded that the majority of the chips in the bag were of the same color as the one drawn. His statement, however, would carry less confidence than an estimate based on a sampling of 100 chips, of which the split in the two colors was about 70–30. The problem concerned the efficiency with which a subject used information in an obtained sample to revise his opinion of the likelihood that he was sampling from a bag that was predominantly blue or predominantly red.

In the actual experiments, a subject draws twelve chips from one of the book bags and then states a judgment (ranging from 0.00 to 1.00) on the likelihood that the sampled bag is predominantly red. One of the results of a series of studies using this method agrees very well with common sense. As the proportion of red chips in a sample increases, there is a corresponding increase in the likelihood judgments that the sampled bag contains predominantly red chips. That is, a sample of 10 red chips and 2 blue chips produces a higher confidence judgment that the bag being sampled contains a majority of red chips than a draw of 6 red chips and 6 blue chips.

However, there is also ample evidence in these studies that subjects do not change their minds as efficiently as they could on the basis of the information they receive from the samples.

Through the use of a principle of probability theory known as Bayes' theorem, an optimal method of revising opinions in the light of new information has been devised. (See Hayes, 1963, Chapter Four for a good introduction to Bayes' theorem.) We presuppose that an individual begins his judgment with some a priori psychological probability that a proposition is correct. In the example above, he may hold an a priori probability of 0.5 that either one of the book bags contains mostly red chips. Then a set of data is obtained that has some calculable probability of occurring on the hypothesis that some alternative figure is correct (for example, that the proportion of red chips in one of the bags is 0.7). The probability of drawing 12 red chips in a row from a bag *hypothetically* containing 70 percent red chips is 0.7^{12}. The probability that 12 consecutive red chips would be drawn from a bag containing (again hypothetically) 30 percent red chips is correspondingly 0.3^{12}. The conclusion from Bayes' theorem would be that a sample of 12 consecutive red chips would mean a probability of nearly 1.00 that the sample bag contains the majority of red chips. Yet very few subjects would state a probability as high as this on the basis of the obtained information.

The same principles may be applied to several more familiar examples. The beliefs that an automobile will start, that a stuck door will open, or that a balky vending machine will operate may be viewed as probabilistic judgments. In each of these cases there is some a priori probability before a series of trials are begun. This probability changes as a function of the outcome of the trials. But the implication of Edwards' experiments is that human beings normally conduct far more than the necessary number of trials to decide what the outcomes will be. An application of Bayes' theorem could same time and tempers for human operators of recalcitrant devices.

A universal finding of research contrasts the operation of Bayes' theorem with the "intuitive" change of opinion of human subjects. Human beings are rarely as efficient as Bayes' theorem in extracting useful information from a sample of observations. In other words, opinion changes in situations similar to the above are very conservative, and they tend to remain close to original probability levels in spite of new information available. Generally people tend to continue in the beliefs they held before the appearance of new evidence, in a way that often leads to discrepancies between their beliefs and the way things are. (See Edwards, Lindman, & Phillips, 1965, pp. 291–311, for a good exposition of Bayes' theorem in application to problems of this type.)

A parallel finding may be seen in research concerning the formation of accurate predictions about persons. After Sarbin's (1944) original studies, it has been repeatedly shown (see Gough, 1962) that the "intuitive" means of extracting predictively useful information from test results, biographical information, and other personal data, is inferior to specified mathematical procedures. Sarbin showed that a precise equation could be written to combine the information from student files (test scores, high school grades, and so forth), resulting in predictions of college performance that were more accurate than the considered judgment of experienced college personnel based upon the same source of information.

A general conclusion is that human beings are consistently less accurate than normative procedures, whenever there exists a precise normative procedure for either changing opinions or forming probabilistic predictions. For those in the professional position of making predictions and discoveries (scientists, engineers, physicians, clinical psychologists), this implies that normative procedures *should* be applied when possible as adjuncts to the process of scientific opinion change. For the man on the street, this conclusion simply means that people are not as accurately informed as they could be on the basis of information to which they are actually exposed.

Assimilation and Contrast

One of the common information-processing tendencies of human beings acts also as a mechanism of conservatism in mind-changing: preexisting beliefs can distort the interpretation of incoming information so that it is congenial with these beliefs. Incoming information may be distorted (1) to give more support to an entrenched belief than it should (*assimilation*) or (2) to deny the relevance of information to the belief (*contrast*) if the information is sufficiently incompatible with it.

Merton (1968) has offered interesting documentation of these processes as they apply to famous scientists, particularly Nobel laureates. He has noted that many famous scientists complain that much of the credit for work done by associates is wrongly attributed to the famous name and not to the deserving unknowns.[2] Similarly, the process of assimilation functions to increase the expectation of importance for articles published by famous names, which are many times more widely read than works of unknown authors, even when the intrinsic merit of the works may be quite equal.

Although Merton does not report on the possibility, contrast would function in the credit attribution process by creating a dissociation between a famous name and an obviously mediocre work emerging from his laboratory. It is likely that the scientific community would attribute such a work not to the famous leader but to his less competent junior colleagues.

[2] Merton coined the term "Matthew effect" to describe this process, based on the following scripture: "For whosoever hath, to him shall be given, and he shall have abundance: but whosoever hath not, from him shall be taken away even that which he hath." (Matthew 13:12)

Hence, the reputation of the established scientist is its own insurance of continuation.

A wide range of data from both psychophysics and social psychology is consistent with the proposition that contrast and assimilation operate as conservative judgmental processes (see Berkowitz, 1960). For example, information received first about a person tends to have an unduly large effect on the formation of a stable impression of that person (see discussion in Brown, 1965, Chapter 12). This seems to be one of the basic mechanisms for the maintenance of prejudicial beliefs about racial groups.

This further illustrates the importance of preexisting beliefs as determinants of the impact of new information. All propositions are not equally susceptible to scientific proof because there are differences in the a priori credibility of those propositions. For example, if an apparently reliable set of data on the existence of ESP or flying saucers were presented, it is likely that the data would have little effect on the scientific community. It might be argued that the findings could be attributed to non-ESP (or non-flying saucer) hypotheses (for example, methodological artifacts or subtle and unwitting forms of ordinary communication) or it might be charged that the data are fraudulent (contrast). (See Hansel, 1966, for an excellent discussion and evaluation of ESP research and its effect on scientific opinion.) Conventional research reports offering no "startling" findings are rarely subjected to this kind of scrutiny. When they *are* subjected to close scrutiny, it is found, at least in psychology, that errors and misinterpretations of findings in research reports are not at all uncommon (Wolins, 1962; Chapanis & Chapanis, 1964).

It is difficult to predict how information that tends to contradict beliefs will be handled, for this appears to depend upon a variety of circumstantial factors. For example, two separate religious sects that had predicted specific cataclysmic occurrences (atomic disasters, the end of the world, and so forth) differed substantially in their reactions when these predictions were shown to be false. Each group was evidently convinced that the world would come to a violent end on a specific date and made manifest its belief by elaborate preparations for the last day. But unlike Noah, when the preparations were completed, no deluge came. One group, described by Festinger, Riecken, and Schachter (1956) emerged from their period of trial with great proselytizing ardor and eagerly sought publicity for their sect—apparently in an attempt to recruit social support for their position. The other group, described by Hardyck and Braden (1962), made no such attempts, but simply interpreted the doom-prophecy as a test of their faithfulness. Fortunately for their fellow man, the group had credited the prophecy and their strong faith forestalled disaster. In both cases, the radically deviant beliefs were substantially maintained; although the mechanisms of conservation differed considerably, they probably corresponded to differences in the cultural milieu.

Sequential Effects in Prediction

The most common paradigm in research on human learning involves the repeated presentation of a set of simple events until the subject knows what to expect on successive trials. A series of words or nonsense syllables, for example, may be presented on a memory drum until the subject can anticipate each word from the previous word on the list.

When uncertainty is introduced into the presentation of a series of events to a subject, some interesting effects occur. The first effect is one that has long been known to professional gamblers: the tendency of players to avoid betting on options that have enjoyed a long run of hits. Similarly, most people would predict tails for a coin that had previously come up heads ten times in a row. This "Monte Carlo" or "gambler's" fallacy is more technically known as a "negative recency effect." A second and opposite effect has also been found: a "positive recency effect" is the tendency to favor in prediction those events which have occurred with most frequency in recent history. An example would be the tendency of gamblers to bet in favor of a temporarily "hot" jockey.

Cohen (1960) and Edwards (1961) have argued—with some experimental support—that the occurrence of positive or negative recency effects depends upon how the events in a series are considered to be caused. Coin flips are events for which the a priori probabilities for two possible outcomes are presumed to be equal. If the outcomes are entirely controlled by "chance," then the general belief in the "law of averages" (that in the long run about 50 percent of the outcomes will be heads) produces a tendency (negative recency) to predict the opposite outcome after a series of identical plays.

Edwards (1961) obtained positive recency effects when subjects had no basis for estimating a priori probabilities, when they estimated, for example, the number of marked cards that would appear in a deck. Under these conditions, the positive recency effect is merely a manifestation of rational (quasi-Bayesean) modifications in probability estimates as a function of experience. If ten marked cards are consecutively drawn from a deck containing an unknown proportion of marked cards, it seems reasonable to expect that the next card will be marked also.

Positive recency may be considered as a case of assimilation, in which predictions are matched with immediately preceding outcomes on the supposition that the system producing the outcomes is biased in favor of those most frequently occurring. Negative recency judgments may be seen as a case of the contrast effect, for predictions are contrasted with the immediately preceding cases on the supposition that chance could not produce a yet longer series of identical outcomes.

Outcomes that are influenced by skill, or by the behavioral intervention of the subject, should be productive of the positive recency rather than the negative recency effect. In ring-toss games, dart games, and other procedures involving fine motoric skills of the subject, the predicted levels of performance are based most strongly on the most recent set of results. (See Rotter, 1954; Cohen & Dearneley, 1962, for experiments on "levels of aspiration" that support this conclusion.) Cantril (1965) has shown that the popular expectations of progress for a nation are based most importantly upon an assessment of how much progress has been made in recent national history. In general, the people of nations that have undergone rapid recent development have the strongest expectations for more progress in the near future.

Recapitulation   No simple answer can be given to the general question of how people change their minds. Man is not a passive register of environmental events, and he does not form expectations purely on the basis of the relative frequency of occurrence of things. It is more appropriate to view man as a builder or constructor of his psychological environment. As such, he appears to have an investment in maintaining his existing constructions; he selects and deploys new information accordingly. Pre-existing expectancies appear to determine the tendencies either to predict that things will continue to happen as they have been happening (assimilation and positive recency, or to predict that recent events are an exception to the rule and will be balanced by the next turn of events (contrast and negative recency). Even normative opinion-changing models, such as the one provided by Bayes' theorem, are based upon the presumption that "starting beliefs" are important as determinants of the impact of information.

Another observation also suggests that the frequency-absorption model is inadequate as a representation of how cognitive structures are formed: Men evidently believe a good deal more than can be accounted for by the "direct evidence of the senses." The common man, as well as the scientist has beliefs that go far beyond the data given.

THE DEVELOPMENT OF VALUES

The values of a newborn infant seem few; food and water, relief from physical discomforts and from internal tensions would seem to be a good inventory of originally valued occurrences. But consider the adult. He has special tastes for food, styles, art and architecture; a sense of the value of tokens of economic exchange, such as money and stock certificates; a conscience and sense of shame or guilt; moral feelings about how men ought to conduct themselves; respect for formalized social laws and respect as well for innumerable unformalized social conventions; profound evaluations of people; and feelings of friendship, love, community.

He also has distastes, or a list of things that disgust him; there are laws he does not respect, people he does not like, and traditional tokens of value which he rejects.

All of these adult dispositions may function as values, influencing decisions and behaviors in the manner described in the previous chapter. What happens in the period between early infancy and adulthood is known in the tradition of psychological research as *socialization*. The influence of society upon the individual is presumed to determine the proliferation and differentiation of values, and the problems touched upon in the last section are also formally within the scope of socialization research. But the primary emphasis of that research is consistent with the aim of this section—to consider the acquisition of human values.

Identification and Imitation

In Chapter I we examined Freud's enormous influence in the psychology of motivation and his affirmation that motivational influences are ubiquitous. But there is greater present relevance in another of Freud's major contributions—the definition of identification as a process of cultural transmission of social values from parent to child (see Freud, 1921). Through identification with parents, particularly with the parent of the same sex, the child was considered to introject, or incorporate into itself, the tastes, rules, and sense of conscience of the parents.

Since Freud's formation of the topic, a good amount of theoretical and empirical controversy has raged over whether identification is a result of a *threatening* parent-child relationship (in which the child identifies with the aggressor as a defense mechanism) or of a *nurturant* parent-child relationship (in which the child is seen as adopting secondary characteristics of targets that he likes). There is evidence for both positions. (See Bronfenbrenner, 1960 for the former, Mischel & Grusec, 1966, for evidence to the latter.) There has also been controversy over the distinction between the processes of identification and imitation; Bronfenbrenner (1960) has defended the position that identification is ". . . a more sweeping and powerful phenomenon" than imitation, whereas Bandura and Walters (1963) have found absolutely no conceptual or empirical distinction between the two.

The issues concern the details of the process of identification and certain matters of terminological convention. (See Mussen, 1967, for a balanced discussion of these and related topics.) Of present concern is the general view presented by this line of research on the social learning of values.

The clearest experimental examples of this process are provided in the works of Bandura and his colleagues. (See Bandura, 1966, for an overall view of this work.) Typical experiments involve children in a playroom setting, models (usually female adults in the role of "teacher"), and some task, problem, or activity. In the course of directing or instructing the child, the model exhibits a critical set of behaviors that are extrinsic to the performance of the task at hand. For example, the model may display bursts of temper and punch or bang objects, or use loud or rude language. Other children are exposed to the same setting without the emission of the critical set of behaviors. The general finding is that the children exposed to the critical set of behaviors tend to exhibit the same kinds of behavioral flourishes as they observed in their models—copying gestures, phrases, and intonation. The control children, of course, do not exhibit these behaviors. It has been shown that a wide variety of behaviors may be acquired in this fashion.

This situation may be taken as the paradigm to illustrate the transmission of social norms that (as discussed in Chapter IV) operate as values in specific behavior settings. If this process were repeated thousands of times and if the evaluative propensities of the models remained as constant as they do in ordinary parent-child relationships, then the results would suggest a fairly good explanation for the frequent observation that children tend to be like their parents (see Sears, Maccoby, & Levin, 1957).

But children can develop very distinguishable values; especially as they become adults, they may depart considerably from the value-patterns laid down by parents. The explanation may be that the adolescent, or becoming-adult, acquires new and more salient self-models, and hence, new values.

Role Models

We will find it convenient again to make use of some of the conceptions of role theory. In role theoretical terms, the behavior of the models in the Bandura experiments functions to instruct a naive actor. He is given a set of expectations associated with a new role; he accepts this definition of the role and performs accordingly when the opportunity is given him to assume the part of the model. Applied now to the parent-child situation, the important implication of role theory (see Mead, 1934) is that the self is formed from the common accumulations of transitory roles. Again, there is an explanation for the similarity of parents and their children, since children are fledgling actors who follow their experienced directors—the parents.

But observation of the behavior of a model is only one of the means by which role-expectations and operative social norms may be developed. There are many other forms of direction, and the studies described below exemplify a few of them.

In a classic study by Liebermann (1956), of individuals in complementary role positions, the differences between attitudes of union men and of management men in a factory were assessed. Liebermann considered the consequences that arose when individuals were transferred from one position to another—union men made supervisors or agents of management, and supervisors made stewards or agents of the union. The effects of these shifts in role on the values of the transferred men were quite dramatic, if predictable. Once they had become union stewards, men changed their attitudes decidedly in favor of labor, and a corresponding shift occurred for those making the opposite transfer. With a touch of research elegance, Liebermann was also able to show that these shifts were reversible. Those who returned to their previous roles reverted to their previous values. In sum, social values were adopted as a function of a shift in roles, with an accompanying difference in the salience of competing role models.

Milgram (1964) supplied another example of the acquisition of social values in his work on the compliance behavior of subjects in psychological experiments. Milgram was interested in determining the extent to which subjects would be willing to perform acts that would seem of questionable "rightness" under most circumstances. The basic set-up for these experiments involved (*a*) the volunteering subject, (*b*) an experimenter, and (*c*) an actor who posed as a second experimental subject. Two separate booths were connected by a common window and electric cables. In the actor-subject's room was a memory drum, and in the naive subject's room a device that was supposedly to be used for administering electric shocks to the actor-subject. Real subjects were instructed to administer electric shocks to the subject in the other room as punishments for incorrect responses on a verbal learning task. Although no actual shocks were administered, the actor responded convincingly to the pseudo-shocks. Gradually, as the number of errors increased, the naive subject was instructed to increase the intensity of the shock, up to and beyond a level marked "Danger" on the dial. When intense pseudo-shocks were given, the actor would plead for relief, claiming a heart condition and convincingly demonstrating considerable pain and anguish. The basic findings of Milgram's work is that most subjects (about 60 percent) were quite willing to proceed with the administration of the very highest shock level. Only a small minority of subjects said that they would not participate in the administration of electric shocks because they "did not approve" of the practice.

The analogy with the German prison camps during World War II is only too clear on several levels. Subjects in Milgram's experiments, when questioned about their behavior, explained it in terms of the instructions that were given them. The experimenter had *asked* them to administer the shocks and had assured them that it was "all right"; otherwise the subject would not have done it, because he "felt bad" about it. Subjects, in a sense, trusted the experimenter not to provide an improper specification of the norms meant to govern behavior in the experiment. Similarly, Nazi soldiers depended upon their superiors to make just decisions concerning prisoner treatment. Carrying out orders is simply a manifestation of that trust—a fulfillment of communicated role-expectations.

Other experiments have shown that individuals in complementary role positions are powerful definers of operative values. Orne and Evans (1965), for example, have shown that a subject can be induced under appropriate experimental conditions to reach into a beaker of fulminating acid for a submerged penny, pick up a venomous snake with his bare hands, or throw acid in the face of another person. (Of course, the experiment was, in reality, perfectly safe.) Orne (1962) has shown that subjects will gladly perform endlessly repetitive tasks when instructed to do so by an experimenter.

In each of the cases cited above, values are defined for new role occupants as part of their initiation into those roles. Consistently, these values then become operative in the *situation for which they were defined*. There is far less direct evidence for the generalization of values acquired in this fashion, but there does exist strong presumptive evidence that persons can be shaped in many ways by extended applications of the principles illustrated in these experiments.

However, we have not yet completed a satisfactory account of the mechanisms of value acquisition. Some individuals refuse participation in experiments of the Milgram type, and others do not seem to be well shaped by the social roles into which they happen to fall. We must examine more closely the transformation of transitory social norms into personal convictions; in particular, we must consider the question of moral development, or the development of ethical principles.

Moral Development

Some of the most striking differences between the values of adults and those of children are moral differences. A child may simply adopt as his moral standards the rules given to him by the commanding adults in his presence, but later he will probably realize that more than one set of such rules exist. At that point the necessity of making choices among values emerges and the child begins to make moral judgments.

At some time prior to adulthood, perhaps most prominently in the period of adolescence, an individual characteristically begins to develop a value system that is qualitatively different from the examples of assimilation presented in the last section. The socialization of the individual involves more than the conformity of behavior to existing norms, as is evidenced by the variety of human societies and by the social change that occurs from generation to generation. The process of socialization produces also an individual who is to some degree a reflector on, and a revisor of, the values of the preceding generation; thus, this individual is also a moralizer.

We find an interesting parallel in the ideas of two seminal twentieth century thinkers on this topic: the Swiss logician-psychologist Jean Piaget (1950) and the American social psychologist George Herbert Mead (1934). Although the main contributions of Piaget have been in the area of cognitive development, and those of Mead in providing the foundations for a thoroughgoing role-theoretical psychology, both of them have considered the critical problem of an individual's moral sense—how he develops ideas of justice, duty, responsibility, cooperation, and obligation.

Society and mind   Both Piaget and Mead consider that the fundamental reality of mind is socially based; that is, they consider that mind is inconceivable outside of a reciprocal social context of development. "Our contention is that mind can never find expression, and could never come into existence at all, except in terms of a social environment" (Mead). "Social life is necessary if the individual is to become conscious of the functioning of his own mind" (Piaget). (Note that the use of the term "mind" in both of these contexts is consistent with the functional position that has been repeatedly emphasized in previous chapters. Mind refers to an evident functional capacity of individuals to think reflectively, symbolically, and abstractly.)

Both writers see evident similarities in the development of cognitive and moral functions. And both agree that a primary fact of cognitive development is the process of "decentering," or the developing capacity of the thinker to consider a problem from a variety of perspectives, not all of them his own. Piaget noted, for example, that very young children (4–5 years old) were unable to describe what a paper-maché mockup of a mountain range would look like from the other side of the table. These children persisted in the belief that all views of reality were like the particular view that happened to impinge upon them. But later, children were able to envision the mountain range as it would look from the other side of the table, without changing their positions. Piaget considers that maturational and social prerequisites are essential for the development of this ability. Without some form of cooperative interaction with other people, the ability to see things from another perspective is greatly inhibited.

The application of this idea to the case of moral development is clearly expressed by Mead: "That which creates the duties, rights, the customs, the laws and the various institutions in human society, as distinguished from the physiological relationships of an anthill or a beehive, is the capacity of the human individual to assume the organized attitude of the community toward himself as well as toward others." (Quoted in Pfuetze, 1961, p. 60.)

The central idea of Mead is the existence of a characteristic evolution in moral development—from automatic adherence to arbitrary rules and compulsory obedience to mandates, to a situation of bilateral respect and cooperation. The latter is based on the ability of the individual to take a broad conception of social functioning or, in Mead's terms, to take the role of the "generalized other."

Piaget has collected interesting data from children who were asked questions concerning the things they regarded as unfair in life. He found that responses fell into four categories:

1. Doing things that are forbidden by adults.
2. Breaking the rules of a game.
3. Behaving in a way that goes against the equality of persons.
4. Acts of injustice associated with adult society.

Examples within these categories are easy to provide, but two statements reported by Piaget are particularly useful. Heading (1) included "Children who make a noise with their feet during prayers," and heading (4) "Children who leave a little girl out of their games, who is not so well dressed as they are." The striking result of these studies was the steady age progression of responses to the "unfairness" question. Young children gave predominant responses in categories (1) and (2), whereas the responses of older children fell into categories (3) and (4). This can be seen in the two statements cited above.

A concomitant development occurs in the regard of children for rules. (These conclusions are based on Piaget's observations of children playing marbles.) Young children regard their rules as sacred, as subject to neither question nor emendation. Older children recognize that rules are a matter of social convention, that a mutual agreement may be modified from time to time to suit the occasion. Again, this is evidence of a "decentering" of moral judgments—of an ability to view situations in a wide social context. Obligatory conformity is replaced by a sense of free cooperation.

Some recent evidence   Some interesting data are reported by Hess and Shipman (1968) on the types of developmental training given by lower-class and middle-class mothers in Chicago. Children and their mothers were involved in an experimental game requiring the reproduction by mother-child teams of simple sketches presented only to the mother. When the child's turn came, the mother was to explain to him how the lines were to be produced. The result was a striking difference in the types of instructions given by the middle-class and lower-class mothers. Lower-class mothers tended to give only literal, imperative instructions. ("Now draw a two-inch line to the left.") Middle-class mothers, by contrast, tried to give their children the general characteristics of the figure to be produced, and to place their instructions for the child's moves in the context of the total production. ("Now you must make the crossbar of an H.") The cooperative behavior of the middle-class mothers fits the characterization by Piaget of the necessary social prerequisite for the development of higher, more decentered thought processes.

Additional evidence is provided by Hess and Shipman on the question of the moral development of middle- and lower-class children. Interviewers found large differences in the types of attitudes expressed toward the schooling of children and in the expectations held by parents for "good behavior" in the schools. Middle-class children, not surprisingly, were given an achievement orientation by their parents. Parents were interested in what the child was learning, in whether the school programs were challenging the abilities of the child, and in how the child was performing in relation to other children. The concern of lower-class mothers for these issues was greatly diminished and was overshadowed by one concern—the extent to which the child behaved well, or "minded the teacher." Similarly, it was found that there was great emphasis in lower-class homes on children behaving themselves, "minding," and not "talking back," with commands taking the form of naked imperatives. Middle-class mothers made a greater effort to explain to their children the "why" of commands and requests, and they attempted to elicit the cooperation of the child rather than his mere compliance.

These data suggest that there is an explanatory mechanism for social class differences in both cognitive abilities and the development of abstract social values (see Mussen, 1967). Such an interpretation should be made with caution, for it is likely that a variety of diverse mechanisms are responsible for these differences. For present purposes, the report of Hess and Shipman supports the theoretical ideas of Piaget and Mead on moral development.

Recapitulation   Moral development appears to be a social process in both origin and effect. Cooperative and reciprocal interactions with others produce an ability to take a social perspective and to view rules not as absolutes but as disputable conventions. From this kind of interaction, a morally autonomous self develops, with characteristic ideas of moral "oughts" (see Scott, 1965).

Moral development may also be seen in relation to the graded series of behavioral "stages" developed in the last chapter. At Stage 5, moral values operate in a consistent, unflexible, and coercive fashion; for a judge at a criminal trial, for example, moral values in this stage are relevant to the tasks of making decisions and implementing actions. But at Stage 6, the self-reflective stage, moral values are a subject of evaluation—the person may consider them, weigh them, and change them (at least for himself) as a result of his reflections. It is to be hoped that the judge in court is more than an implementer of standard moral judgments, that beyond the courtroom he is a reflective and morally "developing" man as well.

RELATIONSHIPS BETWEEN BELIEFS AND VALUES

An intriguing set of psychological issues arises when we consider the relationships that may exist between beliefs and values. Optimism and pessimism, wishful thinking, self-delusion, an attitude of "sour-grapes," and the disposition to think that "the grass is greener" are some of the vernacular references to a causal relationship between beliefs and values. The common tendency to describe values as beliefs ("I don't believe in capital punishment" or the phrase "moral beliefs") and beliefs as values ("I was motivated by the belief that . . .") also suggests a relationship between them.

Coalesced Belief-Values

In considering the last possibility stated above—that beliefs may under some circumstances function as a motive or value—we find an example of such usage in the following quotation from an article by Deese (1962):

> No real substitute for the contiguity-similarity (proto-Lockean) postulate is offered here. The highly organized economy of associative meaning has impressed the author, however, and it was a *belief* that the human mind derived associations from categories of its own *that sent him* (Locke) on the search for a technique by which to study associative meaning. Thus, the least that can be offered is the suggestion that associations derive in whole or part from the structures or categories of the human mind. This *belief* is probably the *mover* of attempts, such as Woodworth's, to classify associations. Such attempts are fruitless, however, for if there are categories of association, they are categories of association, not categories of subordination, coordination, etc. This is admittedly the *belief that motivated* the present work. (p. 174) [Italics added to the original.]

Is this merely a semantic confusion, or can beliefs have motivating properties? How may a belief function as a value? In the case quoted, the belief provides a recognition of a distinct and perhaps novel option. For the scientists, the recognition of a possibility is often the condition for the consummation of pursuit behavior. But must there not be some positive affective significance to a possibility in order for it to be chosen? Must it not be the case that Deese would in some manner "enjoy it" if his interpretation of associative meaning were correct? Perhaps he would, but the specific utility of this confirmation does not depend upon the formal characteristics of Deese's solution, but rather upon the fact that it is *his* solution, *his* contribution, *his* interpretation. Would the scientist, idealized, hesitate in the pursuit of bitter truth?[3]

We achieve some resolution to this problem by rephrasing the matter in terms of social roles. The ultimate goals of the scientist or scholar are defined with these roles—the pursuit and communication of "truth." Movement is therefore determined by possibilities of discovery, and secondary importance is attached to what is being discovered, as long as it is within the subject matter identified with the researcher's role. Thus, a "driven" man may be a man who has a strong and lively vision of the possible. As model airplane builders and sport fishermen know, realizing a vision may be much more fun than living with the realized product of that vision.

In another sense, beliefs seem to be indistinguishable from values, and the clearest example is provided by religions.[4] Beliefs and values seem to have merged at the level of formalized creeds. It is easy to neglect the distinction between a belief in God and a love (valuing) of God. Moral principles that derive from religions, such as the Ten Commandments of the Old Testament or the beatitudes of the New Testament, appear as *objects* of belief even though they take the form of classic value-judgments.

The belief-character of moral values is consistent with Piaget's concept of reflective morality described in the last section, and also with certain conventional philosophical criteria of moral principles. According to Piaget, moral views are adopted *after* a consideration of various kinds of "good." Because there is no way of reducing ultimate values further to other values, the only way to describe such a choice is to state that a particular set of values is the one "believed in." In addition to the quality of irreducibility, the criterion of "universal oughtness" is sometimes applied to moral values. Moral values are ". . . a universal ought toward which all people should strive" (Scott, 1965, p. 15). Such "oughts" are also naturally stated as beliefs ("I believe all men should be charitable").

Psychological research has yet to develop adequate information on the relevance of such coalesced belief-values. It cannot suffice to state that moral principles have little behavioral relevance because people often contradict their stated morals by their actions. The retention of moral belief-values in a majority of men is evidence that some important psychological function is served by them (see Scott, 1965).

"You cherish those predictions that turn out right, even if they are predictions of disaster." (John Kenneth Galbraith, quoted in *Time*, Feb. 16, 1968.)
I am indebted to Professor Sarbin for pointing out that an etymological root of the English word *belief* (galaubon, an old Teutonic word) had a strong evaluative sense, meaning to esteem or to value. This root is also a probable root of the English word *love*.

Value-biased Beliefs and Belief-determined Values

A separate pair of psychological questions concerns the extent to which judgments of value are based on expectancies and the extent to which expectancies are based on judgments of value. The "grass i greener" phenomenon would be an example of the former, in which the value of an object is increased psychologically by virtue of its inaccessibil ity. An example of the second question is "wishful thinking." According to James, "To conceive with passion is . . . to affirm," that is, expectan cies are influenced by values.

The possibility that beliefs and values affect each other in this fashion is not a matter to be settled by flat assumption. In the decision theorie reviewed in Chapter IV, an assumption of independent variation of beliefs and values is frequently adopted as a matter of convenience (see Edwards, 1962); most theorists, however, are also aware that the empirica questions remain open (see especially Rotter, Seeman, & Liverant, 1962) The tactic of current research is to explore the conditions under which beliefs and values are found to be causally related, with a concurren attempt to bring theoretical order into this area by the introduction of qualifying variables.

Beliefs as antecedents to values   The possibility that expectations influ ence values was first stated in a systematic way by Lewin. The subjectiv probability of attaining some objective serves as a cue to the evaluation of that objective, perhaps as a generalization of a consistent ecologica relationship between the difficulty of attaining something and the wortl of that thing. (An example would be the general correlation between the price of commodities and the quality of those commodities.) Atkinsor (1957) has expanded and systematized Lewin's idea in the following way The attractiveness of success is considered to be a function of the difficult of success—if the road has been hard, the fruits of success are sweeter Similarly, the negative value of failing is considered to be a function of how much challenge (probability of failing) was imposed by a task It is presumably more embarrassing to fail at easy tasks than at difficul tasks. (See Lawrence & Festinger, 1962; Atkinson, Bastian, Earl, & Litwir 1960, for confirmatory demonstrations of this relationship.)

Atkinson and his co-workers have suggested that there are consisten personality dispositions to value success and to disvalue failure. (For evi dence to this, see Atkinson, Bastian, Earl & Litwin, 1960.) Some peopl are highly achievement-oriented, and for them the value of achieving th improbable or difficult is augmented. Others have a strong and genera aversion to failure and have been shown to prefer either very easy tasks where they are certain not to fail, or (if forced) difficult tasks for whicl there is very little onus for failing. Hence, variations in the general tendencies to value success and to disvalue failure may account for differences in the extent to which operative values are influenced by factors such as difficulty, price, or probability of attainment.

This qualification tempers the generalization of the Lewin-Atkinson position, and indeed this seems necessary in view of common observations. One implication of the theory would be that money acquired effortlessly, as in welfare programs, doles, allowances, and pensions, would not be as highly valued as money acquired through work. Although there is undoubtedly some truth to this, it is not the *whole* truth. Atkinson's theory implies that easy gains will be evaluated according to the dispositions of individuals receiving the gains. In societies that are less achievement oriented than ours, the meaning of welfare may be a very different matter. McClelland (1961) has provided convincing evidence that the value of success per se must be learned or acquired in the process of socialization. There appears to be no general way in which expectancy variables modify the shape of utility functions. Indeed, there has been some suggestion that the extent to which possessions or attainments are objects of pride depends not upon how *much,* but upon how *little* was done by way of attainment (see Santos, 1966, on Brazilian culture).

The Lewin-Atkinson position implies that the specific utility of gambling may derive from preferences for specific probabilities of play, as if certain levels of risk are preferred. If the value of money increases as the likelihood of obtaining that money decreases, then $10 won in a card game would be worth considerably more than $10 held securely in a wallet or bank. Again, we must generalize carefully; although more pleasure may be attached to the $10 in gambling winnings, the implications for the way in which this $10 will be used are by no means certain.

Values as antecedents to beliefs An equally important and no less complicated psychological problem is to determine the conditions under which conceptions of desirability (values) influence judgments of possiblity (beliefs). Freudian psychology has provided a good documentation of human self-delusion that is, the tendency to construct a view of reality in accord with wishes. But man's beliefs about the way in which the world is fashioned are not completely dictated by his passions—what Freud called the "reality principle" works toward the development of a rationally adaptive view of the ecology. Thus, the problem for theory and research is to delineate the conditions under which the value-biasing of beliefs characteristically occurs.

In the typical paradigm for laboratory research on this problem, expectancy statements are obtained from subjects for outcomes that are differentially valued (usually by means of monetary payoffs); the experimenter then notes the extent to which judgments of expectancies are deflected from "objective probabilities" (or the actual relative frequency of outcomes) by the associated values. Marks (1951), for example studied children who were guessing which of several animal cards would be turned up next in a deck; she found that they predicted most frequently the cards that were designated "winning" cards. More sophisticated laboratory studies of this type have shown a similar result (Irwin, 1960; Crandall, Solomon, & Kellaway, 1958; Scheibe, 1964), and they have suggested some of the specific conditions under which such optimistic prediction are likely to occur.

The present author (Scheibe, 1963) has developed a theoretical scheme that outlines the operation of three such qualifying variables (1) the *control* over outcomes (the skill–chance variable); (2) the *demand* for choice (the availability of a variety of decision options); and (3) the extent to which a subject has been exposed to relevant *information* about the likelihood of events (information level).

Within this scheme, *control* refers to the extent to which a person considers his own skill as the determinant of events. Throwing darts at a board from a distance of ten feet is ordinarily a controllable problem whereas throwing them at the same target from a distance of 100 feet would probably be considered a chance-controlled process. There is considerable evidence for the hypothesis that *skill-controlled* events are more likely to coincide with values than *chance-controlled* events.

This hypothesis acquires considerable interest when the levels of construed control differ from the amount of control subjects actually have over the occurrence of events. It has been demonstrated that individuals differ in the extent to which they consider themselves as agents of control for the events that occur to them. Many magical and superstitious rituals may be seen as attempts to exert vicarious control over events that are otherwise completely ungovernable—such as floods, rains, earthquakes and sickness. In the laboratory, it is possible to create illusions of control over outcomes when in fact no such control exists; the result is a strong correspondence between expectancy statements and outcome values. In one experiment (Scheibe, 1963), subjects were shown to be more optimistic about chance-controlled events that occurred contemporaneously (such as throwing dice) than they were about chance events determined "historically" by a preprogrammed selection device. Despite the intrinsic lack of control for all events determined by chance—whether contemporaneous or historical—it appears that subjects *consider* contemporaneous events susceptible to some measure of control.

The variable of perceived control may account for the common observation that statements about the self tend to be extremely favorable (Edwards, 1957; Crowne & Marlowe, 1964). Many individuals, for example, seem to feel personally beyond the reach of group statistics. Most respondents consider that they are less likely than the average person to have an automobile accident; most smokers, while accepting the relationship between smoking and lung cancer, do not believe that they will contract lung cancer as a result of smoking. Finally, it appears that the control variable supplies an explanation of the observation that individuals report feeling safer in automobiles than in airplanes, and safer when driving a car themselves than when someone else is driving.[5]

The control principle would also appear to explain the presence of the large, mechanically unnecessary handle on slot machines. Although completely automatic (and more efficient) machines have been developed, they are apparently not as appealing as the more "involving," manually operated machine. The feeling of actual control over events associated with the older machine is completely false, but this does not mitigate the psychological importance of feeling a physical connection with the spinning symbols inside the apparatus.

Evidence for the influence of the *demand* variable on the concordance of beliefs with values is less clear. In one experiment (Scheibe, 1964) it was shown that subjects were sometimes forced to make value-biased predictions of simple events because they were not given the option of saying that they didn't know what to predict. In a similar experiment, however, this effect was not statistically significant (Scheibe, 1963).

Using assertions about historical facts and current events, it has been shown that forcing subjects to make true–false judgments when they lack confidence in their replies forces a concordance between preferences and assertions of the truth. It appears that convictions can be made to answer demands for those convictions (Scheibe, 1963).

In every social situation, the range of possible behaviors is sharply restricted by the role-demands existing in the situation. A witness in court is obliged to give direct answers to questions; a consulting psychologist is obliged to make predictions and offer opinions; a politician is obliged to make predictions about the future of his society; or a grant-supported scientist is obliged to arrive at conclusions, though his data may be ambiguous. In each of these examples, the demand for expression could cause distortion in what the person says he believes.

Merton (1957) has argued that the lofty aspirations of the social sciences are not as much generalizations and extensions of past success as they are a capitulation to demands ". . . by policy-makers, reformers, and reactionaries; by businessmen and government men, by college presidents and college sophomores" (Merton, 1957, p. 7). The convictions that develop in answer to these demands, states Merton, "involve the error of supposing that competence means adequacy to *any and all* demands, just or unjust, wise or stupid . . . . Implicitly, it is the sacrilegious

---

[5] Data on these questions are given in Scheibe (1963). A number of statements about the interaction of beliefs and values in the remainder of this chapter are based on data contained in this source.

and masochistic error of assuming oneself to be omniscient. In effect, this belief holds that to admit less than universal knowledge is to admit failure. So it often happens in the early phases of a fledgling discipline that its exponents typically make extravagant claims to having evolved total systems of theory, adequate to the entire range of problems encompassed by the discipline" (Merton, 1957, p. 7).

An interaction between levels of the *information* variable and demands for expression has been found to introduce such value-bias in beliefs. In situations when the information level is high, it is unlikely that demands for expression will force a person toward optimistic errors of belief; when information is lacking, high demand is likely to introduce this effect. Similarly, for the variety of questions to which information is not strictly relevant (metaphysical assumptions, cosmological beliefs, articles of religious faith), resultant beliefs are likely to be strongly related to values.

In 45 assertions of indeterminant correctness or truthfulness ("Flying saucers from other planets have never been near the earth" or "King Arthur was not a real historical figure"), subjects tended to assert beliefs in concordance with their values twice as frequently as assertions that went against their values (Scheibe, 1963). For determinant issues on which subjects were well informed ("Some relationships between cigarette smoking and lung cancer have been established"), the subjects' judgments of the truth or falsity of the assertion were not influenced by values. For determinant assertions about which subjects were less well informed ("Women control less than half of the nation's capital"), judgments of truth tended, again, to concord most frequently with stated preferences about the items. (For all of these items, separate groups of subjects were used to establish the preferences and truth-judgments associated with items.)

The conclusion regarding the determinants of the value-biasing of beliefs may be stated as follows: If subjects correctly perceive the degree of control they have over events, if they are well informed about the past history of those events and about the factors likely to influence them in the future, and if they are allowed full liberty in the expression of their predictions (including the option of saying "I don't know"), then belief statements will be quite independent of values.

To the extent that any of these conditions is lacking, the likelihood is increased that value-biased beliefs will be stated. The optimal condition for the production of value-biased beliefs would be characterized by (*a*) an erroneously construed phenomenal control over outcomes; (*b*) the lack of correct or reliable information about the events (or events for which no evidence is relevant); and (*c*) conditions in which choice options are few and forced, such as the obligation to agree or disagree with some assertion.

Theory-building as a Wishful Enterprise

Since theories, in science, philosophy, or religion are often created (a) when information is lacking, (b) when demand for resolution is high, or (c) when the theorist may feel some degree of control in making things come out like he wants them to, it is highly likely that theories will be highly colored by values. Consider the following set of reflections on this possibility:

> It is (the) search for the meaning of the world which lies at the heart of economics. . . . When the economists were done, what had been a humdrum and chaotic world became a living society with a life history and a meaning of its own. (Heilbroner, 1953, p. 7)

> In order to be able to function at all, everyone must impose an order and regularity on the welter of experience impinging upon him. To do this, he develops out of his personal experiences a set of more or less implicit assumptions about the nature of the world in which he lives, which enables him to predict the behavior of others and the outcomes of his own actions. (Frank, 1961, p. 20)

> Yet we must deal with the world and its inhabitants, and therefore some understanding of it is necessary. In order to integrate the fragments of knowledge we do have and to bring some comprehensible order into the chaos of ignorance and some understanding into the complexity, we often do a peculiar thing—we create a world in our minds and pretend it is the real world. When as scientists we create a substitute world, we term it a theoretical model. (Ghiselli, 1964, p. 4)

> That theory will be most generally believed which, besides offering us objects to account satisfactorily for our sensible experience, also offers those which are most interesting, those which appeal most urgently to our aesthetic, emotional, and active needs. (James, 1890, p. 312)

The point of agreement in these quotations, respectively by an economist, a psychiatrist, a modern psychologist, and a nineteenth century philosopher-psychologist, is that the general constructive work of building a theory is related to purposes to which the theory is meant to answer. Theories bring order, allow prediction, show relations, give direct and intrinsic pleasure as well. Merton's assertion has already been noted—that in the early stages of theory construction serious difficulties may emerge because of the strength of these values of theory.

The scientific character of some theories has nothing to do with how those theories came into existence; it is of little importance whether they were wishful productions or not. The point of distinction between scientific theories and other constructions is the matter of the "vulnerability" of proto-theories to new information. Moreover, the scientist is supposed to have a realistic sense of control that may be exercised over events, and a certain freedom as well from demands for theoretical resolutions that exceed current levels of development in research and thinking. All men make hypotheses, they guess, predict, prognosticate, and try to explain. The scientist is merely a man who has accepted a set of role requirements that constrain him to make this natural human work less vulnerable to value-induced distortions.

SUMMARY

One of the major aims of this chapter has been to show that a psychological analysis of beliefs and values leads to a number of provocative and researchable questions. The issues we have considered in this chapter are certainly not exhaustive of all that are possible. In particular, the question of individual differences in "styles" of thinking (see Kogan & Wallach, 1964) has been slighted. However, the topics considered in this chapter are representative of critical problems for future research on beliefs and values.

Cognitive development, or the development of an underlying structure for operative beliefs, is currently a very prominent area in psychological research. The issue of the degree of cognitive "plasticity" of the developing human being is also a matter of much discussion. It is agreed that some kind of cognitive change occurs over the human life span, but there is very little agreement on the number or descriptions of the stages characteristic of this development. Man is not as effective an extractor of environmental information as he could be, nor is he as effective as some machines and mathematical opinion-changing procedures. In general, the disuse of information for the transformation of beliefs and the operation of information distorting processes (such as assimilation and contrast), function in a conservative fashion—they tend to leave starting beliefs relatively intact. A major question for psychological research is to specify the variables, both personal and ecological, that modify the impact of information on existing belief structures (See Rokeach, 1960, on "Dogmatism"; Luchins & Luchins, 1959, on "Rigidity" for two interesting, if divergent, approaches to this issue.)

The question of the development of values, strongly emphasized in research on human socialization, similarly leads to a variety of problems for investigation. Bandura and his co-workers have recently made major advances toward understanding the processes of imitation and identification, by which a child adopts certain implicit values from the exhibited behavior of models. At the level of role theory, parallels exist between this process and the general provision of norms in specific social settings regarding what is legitimate or proper behavior. Some experiments have demonstrated a remarkable degree of flexibility in the operative values of volunteering subjects. On the other hand, human beings are to some extent autonomous, moral creatures. The individual comes out of cooperative social encounters with the broadened, decentered perspective that appears to be the prerequisite of moral principles, properly so-called.

Another set of research issues develop from the evident possibilities that beliefs may influence values and that values influence beliefs. Optimism and pessimism may be described as distortions of belief statements by the value associated with belief options. The inflation or deflation of values as a product of probability of attainment, price, or effort is an example of the opposite causal sequence. The value of difficult success, or achievement, appears to be an important variable for describing individuals as well as cultures. However, the biasing process seems universal since everyone is in some sense a constructor of beliefs from meager information. In this, scientists are unique in the extent to which they adopt certain rules for keeping beliefs and values apart—not in the setting of problems or initial theories, but in resolution and development of them.

VI

Applications and Extensions

The total world of which the philosopher must take account is thus composed of the realities plus the fancies and illusions.

Wm. James

OVER THE CENTURY of its modern history, psychology has developed a set of traditions to deal with the questions pressed upon it by a curious society. What are the causes of "madness" and how should the condition be treated? What lies behind the common conflict between parent and child? Why do some individuals seem to have no respect for law? How does it happen that a political demagogue may have fantastic powers over the minds of men? What is the psychology of the revolutionary? Why do men gamble, worship, and hold fast to certain superstitutions? Why is man so easily duped and hoaxed? What is necessary for the maintenance of psychological integrity?

With the existing state of psychological knowledge, answers produced for questions of this type are likely to be highly speculative. Speculations, in turn, could lead to attempts at empirical verification, or to the error that the present generation may mistake them for fixed conclusions. To avoid this danger, we must acknowledge that old speculations are always replaceable by newer—perhaps more useful and accurate—hypotheses.

This chapter will attempt to extend the lines of thought described in the previous chapters to some of the problems suggested above. The basic contention is that these problems are particularly tractable to analysis in terms of beliefs and values.

THE CONSEQUENCES OF DEVIANCE IN BELIEFS AND VALUES

A uniformity of beliefs and values results in several positive and functional consequences. Social uniformity of belief means a shared view of reality and increases man's ability to communicate. Similarly, the sharing of values contributes to the predictability of social behavior and strengthens mutual confidence and trust. Thus, such uniformity seems desirable to society and deviations in beliefs and values are often regarded as threatening.

However, many societies value change, variety, liberty, and progress as much as they value stability and order. A conflict comes with the recognition that these ends may only be served by the toleration and encouragement of differences in the ways of interpreting and evaluating reality. Societies are then faced with the problem of dividing "helpful or harmless" deviations from "annoying or harmful" deviations and of devising appropriate social sanctions to implement these distinctions.[1]

"Mental Illness"

The conventional explanation of "madness" offered by psychology has been stated in terms of a metaphor borrowed from the medical profession. Individuals who engage in unusually threatening, strange, or embarrassing conduct are not thought to be demon-possessed, as in an earlier age, but are considered to have sick minds, or "mental illness." Thus, the regulation and supervision of deviant individuals passed, after the Renaissance, from church officials to the medical profession. Sarbin (1967b) offers the following comment on this transformation:

> The 16th century witnessed the beginning of a reaction against the excesses of the Inquisition. The beginnings of Humanistic philosophy, the discovery and serious study of Galen and other classical writers, the renunciation of scholasticism—the whole thrust of the Renaissance was opposite to that of the Inquisition. In this atmosphere, Teresa of Avila, an outstanding figure of the Counter-reformation, contributed to the shift from demons to "illness" as the cause of conduct disturbance. A group of nuns were exhibiting conduct which at a later date would have been called hysteria. By declaring these women to be infirm or ill Teresa was able to fend off the Inquisition. However, the appeal that a diagnosis should be changed from witchcraft to illness required some cognitive elaboration. She invoked the notion of *natural* causes. Among the natural causes were (a) melancholy (Galenic humoral pathology), (b) weak imagination, and (c) drowsiness. If a person's conduct could be accounted

---

[1] The fields of art and literature provide interesting examples of this process. Fellowships, prizes, and awards serve as rewards for positive deviations, while censorship, official castigation, or political imprisonment serve as negative sanctions. That there are differences among societies in how the harmful is divided from the harmless is attested by the recent trials in Russia of young intellectuals whose works are simultaneously honored and cheered in the West. It is the beliefs and values which these works manifest, rather than the surface of the art, that causes so much trouble.

for by such natural causes they were to be regarded not as evil, but *comas enfermas, as if sick*. By employing the metaphor—as if sick— she implied that practitioners of physik rather than clergymen should be the responsible social specialists. (p. 448)

Humanitarian values were behind the efforts of Teresa of Avila and those of her nineteenth-century counterpart, Dorothea Dix, in their suggestion that sickness rather than evil is the responsible agent for grossly deviant conduct. There is ample basis for the contemporary rejection of this notion—for the same humanitarian reasons. The practical objection is that the grouping of behavioral disorders, which are necessarily socially relative, with physical disorders, which are not, has been functionally inadequate; effective cures for such behavioral disorders have not been developed and existing remedies are at best irregular in their success (see Shaver & Scheibe, 1967). Moreover, a variety of authors have documented the possibility that labeling a person as "mentally ill" is permanently degrading and socially stigmatic (Goffman, 1961; Talbot, Miller, & White, 1964; Sarbin, 1967b; Szasz, 1961). This effect is precisely opposed to the intentions of the original reformers.

The philosopher Gilbert Ryle has said that, "To explode a myth is not to deny the facts but to re-allocate them" (1949, p. 8). Thus, there is no denying the existence of the socially consequential deviant behaviors that traditionally result in the imputation of mental illness. On occasion, individuals do "run amok" on apparently senseless sprees of destruction, report unusual and bizarre visions, and in other ways break the "norms of propriety" within a society. But to categorize such behaviors as symptoms of mental illness is to direct attention for their etiology to the inward mental (psychic) dispositions of the person. As we have seen, there is functional legitimacy in referring to "mind" as process. But, to talk about mind in *other* than a metaphoric sense as something that can be "sick" or "healthy" is to create an unfortunate myth.

The analysis of behavioral deviations from social norms requires the same sort of terms as the analysis of any other kind of behavior, with a special attempt to distinguish the antecedents best accounting for the discrepancies. In this book, we have explored antecedents for behavior in terms of beliefs and values as they are called into operation in specific social (role) settings. How might beliefs and values help to explain the facts of "mental illness"?

Discrepancies in social values   If an individual has been socialized according to a different set of values than those applying to the dominant social reference group in his behavior setting, then the person is likely to engage in behaviors that seem "symptomatic." From time to time, there have been strong appeals that individuals engaging in homosexual activities be considered sick, although this same kind of behavior might be (and has been) otherwise construed as a harmless manifestation of individual preference. Recent changes in laws about homosexuality in Great Britain reflect a shift in official value judgments on this matter.

Discrepancies in belief systems   It is characteristic of some systems of belief that behaviors are expected and considered normal which are by psychiatric conventions regarded as cardinal symptoms of mental illness. We find examples of such behavior in the reporting of visions. Rogler and Hollingshead (1961) offer the following observations on spiritualism as one such belief system:

> Persistent hallucinations to the believer in spiritualism are not symptoms of a deranged mind experiencing things unperceived by others—a definition which serves to isolate the sick. Rather they demonstrate the development of psychic facilities that may eventually put the lucky person in more permanent contact with the invisible world. Thus, participation in a spiritualist group serves to structure, define, and render behavior institutionally meaningful that is otherwise perceived as aberrant. (p. 21)

The present author has made similar observations of "macumba" services in Brazil. I discovered that a hotel elevator operator, whom I had encountered and spoken with daily for more than two weeks, was one of the "stars" of a particular "macumba" meeting. There he was distinguished for his ability to translate direct conversations between supplicants and the saint who came to possess him during his trance. In the context of the "macumba" meeting, such behavior was highly valued.

Unequal application of sanctioning rules   Sarbin (1967a) has argued that special internal visions are not unique to those labeled "mentally ill." It appears, instead, that those who report such visions in an inappropriate manner or in circumstances in which others are especially sensitive to "symptoms of mental illness" suffer the unfortunate consequence of being considered mentally ill. Faulkner, for example, told his biographer, Malcolm Cowley, that he wrote by "listening to the voices," and the Brazilian author Guimaraes Rosa asserted that all of his characters were not his creations but were revealed to him from paranormal sources. And in some religions, certain visions are reported as "real" or "authentic." Sarbin offers the following conclusions regarding the diagnosis of hallucinations:

> What are the observations actually employed by professional diagnosers in making a decision that a reported imagining is an hallucination and probably a 'symptom' of schizophrenia?—The answer to this question must come from an examination of the total context in which the label

is used. In the first place, professional judges are generally not required to pass judgments on reported imaginings of representative samplings of a population. Rather, they are called upon to construct inferences and to pass judgments on certain kinds of people—on people who in the first instance are referred by relatives and neighbors or delivered by law-enforcement officers. The diagnoser then has some extrapsychological facts (often prejudiced) which he takes into account when he draws conclusions and passes judgments about imaginings. The first reason for referring or bringing the client to the professional is that the client has engaged in some overt conduct that is disturbing to those that referred him. Such conduct may be conceptualized as the nonfulfillment of ascribed social roles, the violation of propriety norms, and the like. A prediagnosis has already been made as an entry to the professional. The professional judge knows that his client is supected of being mad, crazy, or psychotic, or is a member of an esoteric or primitive society. Such information is a cue that the suspect occupies a degraded position in the social structure. In this condition, then, the term hallucination is ready to be applied to reported imaginings. (1967a, pp. 378–379)

An alternative view   Elsewhere (see Sarbin, Scheibe, & Kroger, 1965), it has been argued that individuals who are currently regarded as mentally ill might more legitimately be regarded as persons with negatively transformed social identities, or as socially degraded individuals. The transformation of social identity is held to be a process of continual transaction between the behaving person and the variety of reference groups to which he is exposed. Deviant behaviors are seen as unsuccessful attempts to cope with stresses as they are translated by the beliefs and values of the person. Thus, the analysis of deviant behaviors demands full attention to the social context in which this person is acting, as well as to his beliefs and values and those of the individuals who are in complementary role positions.

Goffman (1961) has noted that the current system of mental hospitals is not as much an organized attempt to cure individuals who are sick as it is a means of segregating devalued individuals from society. Consistent with this, we know that permanent residents of mental hospitals are largely individuals from minority, recent immigrant, and lower socioeconomic status groups, and that mental patients (and incarcerated prisoners) tend to be of lower intellectual ability than nonpatient populations.[2]

Environmental explanations of "mental diseases" such as paranoia and schizophrenia may emerge when appropriate social investigations are made. Thus Lemert (1962), in a careful examination of the living environments of diagnosed paranoids, discovered a characteristic pattern of *actual*

---

[2] See Hollingshead and Redlich (1958) and Weinberg (1967) on the relation of social and demographic variables to mental hospitalization. See Woodward (1955) on the relation of criminality to intelligence, and Goffman (1961; 1963) for views on other social factors contributing to hospitalization and incarceration.

threat (for job, reputation, or wife) for these individuals considered to have irrational fears. Similarly, it has been shown that the environmental background of schizophrenics is characterized by a high degree of emotional ambivalence toward the prepatient, a pattern of ambivalence that is internalized into the person's conception and evaluation of himself (Bateson, Jackson, Haley, & Weakland, 1956).

From this perspective, the basic problem of psychotherapy is to restore positive social value to the degraded person. Psychotherapy must be conducted in a setting that allows the individual to gain respect and esteem from others, whereas permanent residence in a mental hospital works precisely against this objective.

Anomie and Alienation

The sociologist Durkheim (1897) originated the concept of *anomie* in his classic studies on the relation of social factors to suicide. In Durkheim's system, anomie logically occupies the same position as Tolman's intervening variables (such as cognitive maps). It is a condition thought to derive from a certain combination of social conditions (such as the amounts of industrialization and of family cohesion) and is in turn considered to increase the likelihood of deviant acts, such as suicide. Substantively, Durkheim considered anomie to be a condition of normlessness, or a separation of groups of individuals from a set of stable cultural norms or values. The causes of anomie were associated with the persistence of dominant trends in the history of Western cultural institutions, such as those of church, family, and work group.

Merton (1957) has shown the close relation of the concept of anomie to beliefs and values.[3] Anomie is considered to be a product of the disjunction of values (goals) and of expectations for the legitimate achievement of those values (means). Today, for example, television and magazines communicate much information about goods and qualities that form one set of cultural ideals—automobiles, chic clothing, electronic appliances, travel, and security. Within lower-class urban culture, however, information is also supplied from the immediate environment about the limited possibilities of obtaining these objectives through legitimate means. Poor schools, limited job opportunities, ill health, the presence of "threats" in the form of the police and majority groups, and the examples of previous generations—all serve to create a solid expectation that socially legitimate means cannot correspond with the attainment of the valued goals that are so palpably present. The result, for groups of individuals in these conditions, is anomie. The occurrence of various types of deviant behavior—social revolution, social withdrawal ("mental illness"), criminal

---

[3] Jessor (1962) has described the close relation between Merton's views and a conception of deviant behavior growing out of Rotter's (1954) social learning theory.

activity, or the rejection by certain individuals of their identification with an oppressed group ("passing for white," for example)—depends upon the manner in which individuals cope with anomie.

Merton's formulation also implies that conflicting standards of value may lead to anomie and consequently to movement toward deviant behavior. For this possibility, it is important that we consider the *objective referents* of anomie and deviation. While anomie means the separation from or rejection of a set of cultural norms, it does not follow that an individual who is "anomic" with respect to one set of norms will be completely without norms of any sort. A young "hippie" who rejects the norms of what is seen as the dominant "establishment" in the United States still adopts norms, but they may be the norms of a new reference culture—those of the "hippie" or the "new generation" culture.

The same argument applies to alienation, which has been conventionally described as the psychological counterpart of the sociological concept of anomie. Alienation, or "otherness," similarly implies a separation of the individual from the norms of some reference group. When a person is described as alienated, it makes sense to ask, "Alienated from what?" From his college? From his girl-friend's family? From his mother? From the "establishment"? As long as a person continues to use any we-they distinction, he is not completely separated from all social reference groups. Indeed, considering again the position of Mead on the social origin of self, it is reasonable to question whether someone who is completely alienated from all forms of social reference can legitimately be called a person.

To some degree, everyone is a victim of social alienation. We can regard members of the "establishment" as being alienated from members of a "hippie" culture, and, by default, as alienated from countless other sets of cultural norms with which they could potentially form connections. A society such as our own must be considered "pluralistic" in that it possesses, and ideally tolerates, a large number of somewhat unique belief-value systems. To live in a pluralistic society necessarily involves "alienation" from most of the elements that comprise the plurality, but an individual is likely to *think* of himself or others as alienated only when the group or system that is the object of alienation becomes especially salient. Thus, when a very large and conspicuous entity, such as the United States Government, acts in a way that demonstrates the deviance of its principles from those of a large number of individuals, the awareness of alienation seems acute and unavoidable.

The most difficult part of the argument relating anomie or alienation to acts of social deviance concerns the transition from the condition of a frustrating disjunction of goals and legitimate means to the selection of forms of deviance. As Barker (1965) has shown, it is theoretically neat but empirically wrong to state that frustration is bound to result in a single kind of adaptive response (for example, aggression). Merton has mentioned a variety of the adaptive mechanisms to anomie (rejection of institutionalized means, for example, crime; rejection of goals, for example, passive withdrawal), but it is not clear theoretically what determines that a person choose adaptive device *A* over adaptive device *B*. Cross-cultural comparisons add further complications, for part of the rules that define a culture evidently concerns the measures that *may* be taken by individuals in a condition of alienation from the dominant culture.

We may find no better solution to this problem than the specification in detail of the decision problem facing the individual who is in such a condition. The resulting description would be similar to a collective case study—it would be a portrayal of the live options, the belief-premises, and the values pertaining to a group of individuals in common condition.

Wretched of the earth, written by the Algerian psychoanalyst Franz Fanon (1965), is a good example of such a study. Fanon expresses here the profound sense of alienation that the Algerians felt from the dominant culture of colonial France. More generally, all colonial or quasi-colonial powers are seen collectively as "other," and all colonized and "native" peoples of the earth as "we." The book examines the psychological condition of these people; it provides precisely the information necessary for predicting what adaptive (or deviant) options will be taken by the colonized, *if Fanon's description is correct:*

> From birth it is clear to him (the peasant, the native) that this narrow world, strewn with prohibitions, can only be called in question by absolute violence. (p. 31)

> There is no native who does not dream at least once a day of setting himself up in the settler's place. (p. 32)

> No conciliation is possible, for of the two terms (settlers and natives), one is superfluous. (p. 32)

> The interests of one (of the natives) will be the interests of all. (p. 38)

From these and a few other premises about this condition, clear behavioral predictions emerge. Sartre, in his preface to Fanon's book, comments on the implications as follows:

> This new man [the native who revolts] begins his life as a man at the end of it; he considers himself as a potential corpse. He will be killed; not only does he accept this risk, he's sure of it. This potential dead man has lost his wife and his children; he has seen so many dying men that he prefers victory to survival; others, not he, will have the fruits of victory;

he is too weary of it all. But this weariness of the heart is the root of an unbelievable courage. We find our humanity on this side of death and despair; he finds it beyond torture and death. We have sown the wind; he is the whirlwind. The child of violence, at every moment he draws from it his humanity. We were men at his expense, he makes himself a man at ours: a different man: of higher quality. (pp. 19–20.)

Because of the history of events in Algeria, these statements appear very prophetic; they would apply as well to the case of Vietnam. But the applicability of this line of thinking to every colonized culture is somewhat disputable, and very likely it is not feasible in all cases. The Hawaiian Islands were once a colony, as was Brazil, but the history of decolonization in these cases was a very different matter. Psychology must wait for cultural-historical developments to supply the specific beliefs and values necessary for an analysis of such a problem.

Deviations in Political Behavior

In recent years an important change has taken place in the study of politics, bringing some urgency into the task of developing a correspondence between the concepts and vocabulary of psychology and the problems of political science. The change might be described as the transformation of the study of politics to a "behavioral science," with a strong concern for the systematic description, explanation, and prediction of all behavior that qualifies as political (see Lane, 1963). Consequently, the political scientist has turned to his colleague in psychology with the hope of borrowing some insights and methods. Two recent attempts to survey the results of this admixture support the conclusion that political scientists are not altogether satisfied with what they are able to borrow from psychology (Lane, 1963; Greenstein, 1967).

The subject of politics consistently evokes strong value statements, as is evidenced by an array of terms denoting values as well as items of political vocabulary; freedom, justice, liberty, equality, power, and legality may serve as examples. Moreover, politics is characterized by a variety of organizational systems, which for the individual take the form of competing political creeds. Monarchy, oligarchy, socialism, and various forms of democracy comprise a set of alternative means for the attainment of social goals, which may be widely shared. Further warrant for the mention of political behavior in connection with beliefs and values is found in the observation that the political evolution of laws is perhaps the most obvious codification of a society's changing values. The enforcement of laws—the problem of deviations from laws and from the political systems they represent—brings up the question of the power relations between the individual and the state, and with this question, many other belief-value considerations. The example of Fanon quoted above serves well to illustrate how the beliefs and values of a people may be influenced by systems of political control. These beliefs and values, in turn, may then function to support the violent and deviant action of political revolution.

But we are mistaken if we expect psychology, as a discipline, to provide the behavioral explanations for political acts—if we "reduce" political science to psychology. What emerges from this error is the employment in political science of the theoretical idiom of certain psychological theories (in the past, mainly psychoanalysis) that were developed for a much more circumscribed range of application (for the treatment of the so-called neuroses, for example). Another difficulty in developing useful psychological analyses of political behavior arises when we consider psychology as exclusively concerned with "inner" determinants of behavior. Thus, explanations of political behavior will be found in terms of "inner" and "deep" psychological factors, such as authoritarianism, compulsivity, unresolved unconscious conflicts, or aggresivity. By forcing causal factors into the depths of the psyche (and out of sight) and by coining special names for these factors, the strong impression of psychological explanation may be obtained, when at best the product should be viewed as a somewhat distorted redescription of the events to be explained.[4]

An interactive model of behavior, such as that described in Chapter IV, seems more appropriate for application to political behavior. Thus, the political actor, whether he is the legislator, voter, revolutionary, or president of a nation, is seen to decide upon his political act as a function of the beliefs and values that become salient in each type of decision setting. Salient beliefs and values, in turn, are a product of the interaction between dispositions that the actor brings with him and the demands imposed by the situation.

Thus, the paramount tasks of political psychology are special cases of the major problems of any type of psychology: To discover how people acquire and change their political beliefs and values (for example, diffusion of influence and opinion leadership, Lasswell, 1948; political socialization, Hyman, 1959) and to develop through extensive observation some systematic knowledge of how specific beliefs and values are crystallized and translated into behavior by the "catalytic" action of the political ambience. But the terms of political psychology must be *sui generis:* the types of beliefs and values that operate for political behavior will be to an extent unique to that level of behavior.

---

[4] For some idea of the arbitrariness of this exercise, see two rather divergent psychoanalytic treatments of Woodrow Wilson (Freud & Bullit, 1966; and George & George, 1956).

Consider again the case of the incipient revolutionary. The following observations by Hoffer (1951), whether or not they are correct, seem of the type demanded for the psychological understanding of political acts:

> For men to plunge headlong into an undertaking of vast change, they must be intensely discontented yet not destitute, and they must have the feeling that by the possession of some potent doctrine, infallible leader or some new technique they have access to a source of irresistible power. They must also have an extravagant conception of the prospects and potentialities of the future. Finally, they must be wholly ignorant of the difficulties involved in their vast undertaking. Experience is a handicap. The men who started the French Revolution were wholly without political experience. The same is true of the Bolsheviks, Nazis and the revolutionaries in Asia. The experienced man of affairs is a latecomer. He enters the movement when it is already a going concern. It is perhaps the Englishman's political experience that keeps him shy of mass movements. (p. 20)

The truth-value of speculations of this sort is a highly important matter and lends itself to empirical analysis. The advantage of allegations of this type is that they are subject to falsification. It is not an insuperable task to measure "intense discontentment" (see Cantril, 1965), to determine whether a group has faith in some special "messiah" leader, who is perhaps also inexperienced, and then to note the concurrence of these observations with attempts at political change.

The content of political systems is both the product of social change and a major determinant of beliefs and values adopted by individuals living under that system. For example, beliefs about the self in the United States probably derive in part from the Constitution and the Bill of Rights. These instruments are the effective source of such ideas as "I'm as good as anybody else," and "I'm free to say what I think." In addition, certain values or aspirations for individual attainment are closely modeled after political conventions. Social mobility in American society is both sanctioned by the political arrangement and adopted as a goal by a large proportion of the population.

Finally, as previously noted, the delineation of inadmissible deviations is largely a matter of established legal-political convention. "Mental illness," embodied as "insanity," has a legal meaning which is probably more resistant to change than the technical meaning of the term. Every legal system provides the norms with respect to which socially deviant acts acquire their meaning—through the criteria it announces for dividing the sane from the insane, the criminal from the noncriminal, the franchised from the disenfranchised.

UNCERTAINTY, HOPE, AND DOUBT

The occurrence of "mental illness," the oppressive force of social anomie and alienation, and the constant fluctuations of the political standards erected by man for his own governance seem to be among the by-products of a singularly uncertain and flexible method of living that has evolved with the human species. Much of the fascination for man's study of himself comes from his ability to change his environment and to create—by mental as well as physical construction—new "cultures" in which to live. Thus, the advantages and disadvantages of being human probably derive from the same source: Man is the most intelligent of animals, but he is also the only really stupid animal—all other animals seem to bear their dumbness with a certain dignity. In this section we will attempt to show how certain types of human errors and eccentricities may be related to fundamental adaptive capacities of man.

Superstitions[5]

If we accept the common view that superstitions are the mistaken beliefs of other people, then the concept may seem too familiar to be of much interest. Upon examination, however, this familiarity acquires a fascinating strangeness.

A superstition may be regarded as a special kind of expectation (or subjective probability, hypothesis, premise, or belief). A superstition may be said to exist whenever an individual persistently or repeatedly behaves as if his subjective estimate of the result of that behavior is significantly different from an objective (scientific) estimate of the effect of that behavior. Questions that deserve examination regarding these special expectancies include the following: Some people carry charms and amulets, consult astrologers and palmists, and some do not. What determines wheher or not an individual subscribes to a given superstition? Is it simply that some people are superstitious and others are not? Or may it be said that everyone is superstitious in like degree, with only the specific content of the superstition varying from individual to individual and from group to group? That intelligent college students subscribe to numerous superstitions has been demonstrated (Gilliland, 1930; Dockeray & Valentine, 1935). Is it not appropriate to describe the postulates of scientific theoreticians and of theologians as somewhat highly evolved superstitions?

We must refer once again to the *psychological* problem of epistemology (Chapter II). How do we come to know what we know? What is

[5] This section is essentially a summary of a previous article on superstitions (Scheibe & Sarbin, 1965). Portions of the text of this paper are incorporated directly into the present section without further specific citation.

the relation of the real world to the known world? How do we know *that* we know? Hume argues that cause and effect relationships are not ultimately compelled upon us *in toto,* but that they are inferences based upon contiguity. He says in his *Treatise of Human Nature:* "We find only that the effect does, in fact, follow the cause. The impact of one billiard ball upon another is followed by the motion of the second. There is here contiguity in space and time, but nothing to suggest necessary connection." Yet, it is often overlooked that although this inference be logically unnecessary, it is psychologically very powerful. Cause and effect relationships are psychologically compelled upon us *in toto.* (See Heider, 1944; Michotte, 1963; and Piaget, 1955, for experimental demonstrations of causal inferences.) In short, it is possible to believe that the known world is the real world, and to act as if it is, even though it might be impossible to be ultimately correct in this belief.

A conceptual scheme for superstitions may be stated as follows: Superstitions arise because of an imperfect knowledge of antecedent-consequent relationships in the ecology. On the assumption that an elaborate and fairly definite set of beliefs is *necessary* to support active behavior, superstitions "fill the gap" between the objective probability estimates available to a person and the degree of subjective probability required to execute behaviors. The beginning fact is objective uncertainty. In the face of this uncertainty, beliefs must be adopted so that man is not transfixed for lack of "truth"—when he lacks truth and needs it, he must somehow invent it.

In an experiment with pigeons, Skinner (1948; also, Morse & Skinner, 1957) has demonstrated the means by which a "sort of superstition" is developed. Using his operant conditioning technique, he was able to establish firmly the behavior patterns that happened to precede the presentation of the reinforcement. The bird made swiping motions with its head, behaving as if "there were a causal relation between its behavior and the presentation of food, although such a relation is lacking" (Skinner, 1948, p. 170). The superstitious rituals are due not only to "the fact that a reinforcing stimulus strengthens any behavior that may happen to follow, even though a contingency has not been explicity arranged, but also to the fact that the change in behavior resulting from one accidental contingency makes similar accidents more probable" (Morse & Skinner, 1957, p. 308).

As a prime example of primitive "parataxic" thinking, Sullivan quotes a similar case portrayed in one of Franz Kafka's short stories. A dog who lived in a kennel surrounded by a high fence was urinating one day when a bone was thrown over the fence. The dog thought, "My urinating made that bone appear." Thereafter, whenever he wanted something to eat he lifted his leg.[6] Sullivan believes that much thinking does

---

[6] This example is taken from Hall and Lindzey (1957).

not advance beyond the level of parataxis; that we see causal connections between experiences that have nothing to do with one another. An essential feature of these illustrations is that the animals mentioned misrepresent accidental contingencies as essential contingencies. There is, of course, a wealth of anecdotal human evidence that fits the same description. For example, (from Diprose's *Anecdotes of curious superstitions and omens*):

> In Devonshire, the appearance of a white-breasted bird has long been considered an omen of death. This belief has been traced to a circumstance said to have happened to the Oxenham family in that county, and related by Howell, in his Familiar Letters; wherein is the following monumental inscription: Here lies John Oxenham, a goodly young man, in whose chambers, as he was struggling with the pangs of death, a bird with a white breast, was seen fluttering about his bed, and so vanished. He died immediately. The same circumstances are related of his sister Mary, and two or three others of the family.

The paradigm is the same. First, there is the condition of uncertainty regarding a highly valued outcome: Skinner's pigeons were uncertain of when or whether they were going to be fed, and John Oxenham's relatives were uncertain of when or whether John would expire. Then, immediately prior to the revelation of the outcome, something fortuitous happened. Moreover, the fortuitous pairing of events was repeated at least once. Since both the pigeon and the Oxenhams were ignorant of any more powerful causal agent the fortuitous events were taken as causes. In the future, the pigeon will make swiping motions with its head, and the Oxenhams will avoid white-breasted birds. The same is true of Kafka's dog, which will raise its leg at inappropriate times.

Although this type of explanation accounts for the origin of a superstition in an individual, it does not consider the wide-scale dissemination of superstition. The populace of Devonshire assumed the white-bird superstition, but it is not probable that the entire colony of pigeons adopted the motions of Skinner's subjects.

At this point, we should examine a warning made long ago by Jastrow (1900) regarding the development of superstitions. He warned against the practice of analogical reasoning, against the inference of a further degree of resemblance from an observed degree of resemblance. Jastrow argued that many superstitions, in particular voodoo practices, derive from this faulty logic. Sarbin, Taft, & Bailey (1960) have formulated the process of analogical mediation as follows:

A has characteristic X.
X and Y are defining characteristics of species M.
Therefore, A has characteristic Y and is a member of species M. (p. 62)

Although the conclusion reached here is obviously false, voodoo priests persist in the belief that mutilation of the representation of a person will do harm to that person. Similarly, our more primitive comparative psychologists persist in the belief that what is true of learning in the rat is also true of human learning.

The majority of human superstitions are left quite unexplained. Skinnerian conditioning involves the empirical contiguity of the perceived cause and effect for each individual who bears the superstition, but there seems to be something else involved in the ways people acquire superstitions. For human beings, the first-order demonstration of the efficacy of a superstition is not necessary; that is, one need not be witness to the original contiguity between the fortuitous event and the outcome. For example, Leonardo da Vinci, in "The Last Supper," painted Judas Iscariot in the act of knocking over the salt-cellar. This is held to be the origin of our current superstition that it is bad luck to spill salt, although most people are probably not aware of its origin.

Similarly, astrological superstitions may have had their origin in the fortuitous pairing of a given stellar orientation and a particularly noteworthy earthly event. Such origins are buried in antiquity, yet people continue to be superstitious about the positions of the stars and planets. Popular astrology has, in fact, enjoyed a recent boom and revival. Lewinsohn (1961) offers the following speculation on this phenomenon:

> While the revolution which has been changing the Newtonian world picture ever since 1900 has made some people more skeptical, it has simply made others more credulous. Scientific laws which our textbooks have taught us to look upon as eternal truths have collapsed like ninepins, and new ones still lack the authority that their predecessors enjoyed. Scientists have grown a little more circumspect and no longer dare to proclaim general laws with the facility of their 19th century predecessors. Because of these developments, laymen have begun to feel that it is impossible to distinguish truth from hypothesis. Now laymen have always been sticklers for certainty, and where truth is uncertain, they will accept anything that is presented as being simple and sure. (pp. 93–94)

We might suggest that the current resurgence of mysticism in psychology, as exemplified by some of the existential psychologies, and the popular issue of "consciousness expanding" or psychedelic drugs, might be traceable to the lack of definitive statements within the field of psychology, to disillusionment with psychoanalytic absolutes, and perhaps to a great difficulty of understanding the rather sophisticated mathematical orientations of some of the new developments in psychology.

The simplest declaration on the problem of acquisition of superstitions should not be avoided: That is, people may acquire their superstitions by direct verbal communication, as well as from the first-hand perception of fortuitous pairing of events. It is as if each culture presents its participants with a rule book stating standard beliefs about what leads to what. These standard beliefs may be regarded as major premises that stand ready—under conditions of uncertainty—to place or identify cognitively a potentially threatening or disturbing event in such a way as to bring it under control.

Gambling

In the last chapter, we observed that some types of play with uncertainty may be of intrinsic value.[7] In view of this, there is perhaps another function of superstitions beyond the creation of cognitive order and the facilitation of more confident actions. Superstitions may be "extra beliefs" created to provide material for hope and doubt in a world of too much certainty. From this we can conclude the possibility that gambling and superstitions are related in their psychological functions.

The functional significance of gambling is evidenced by its ubiquity in cultures and throughout history. Gambling is mentioned in the Bible, the Talmud, and the Koran, by Aristotle, and by the cryptic messages left by ancient Egyptians (see Cohen, 1960). There is also some uniformity in the identification of gambling as a vice; laws and injunctions against gambling seem as common as the practice itself. The recent trend toward liberalized gaming laws, as part of efforts to draw tourists or to provide a source of public revenue, has produced a revival of the classical reform arguments about the evils of gambling.[8] Evidently society has achieved no stable set of legal-moral conventions for the regulation of gambling behavior.

There are two types of feasible explanations for the persistence of the apparently paradoxical (and counter-productive) form of behavior represented in gambling. Either individuals mistakenly believe that they can win at gambling when they cannot, or else the values involved in gambling are not well represented by monetary gains and losses.

---

[7] "Certainty is the root of despair. The inevitable stales, while doubt and hope are sisters. Not unfortunately, the universe is wild—game-flavored as hawk's wing." (Blood, in *The Anesthetic Revolution.*) This is quoted, in the present case, from Cantril (1965).
[8] A British government official expressed his disappointment with the new gaming laws as follows: "There are families whose lives are being made a hell because of gambling. The time has come to strike a note of warning to the nation. Unless a halt is called we will be on the way to decadence from which it will be very difficult to recover." At nearly the same time that this statement was made, a bank teller was discovered to have embezzled $11,000, most of which he had lost playing roulette at London casinos (United Press International, January 16, 1966). Cohen (1960) was drawn to the psychological study of gambling because he began wondering why so much labor remained allocated to the gambling industry in Britain during the war when there was a critical shortage of productive manpower.

The first type of explanation suggests that the formation of expectations in gambling may be a case of value-biasing, as described in the last chapter. If this is the case, gambling should be most common (a) when information or experience with specific gambling situations is lacking, (b) when the illusion is great that some kind of skill is involved in winning (pulling a slot machine lever, picking the horses "scientifically"), and (c) when there is pressure or "demand" for a person to make a clear decision either to gamble or not to gamble. The level of all three of these variables would be most conducive to gambling for the tourist landing for the first time in Las Vegas and faced with the decision of whether or not to deposit his change in the waiting slot machines. The levels of these variables would also be high for the race track neophyte, whose illusion of skill may be encouraged by the purchase of a tout sheet or racing form.

However, this does not yet explain the case of the habitual gambler, who gambles despite himself and with ample informational basis for expecting to lose. In this case, we must look for values other than those posted with winnings and losings.

For these special values of gambling there are many possibilities, some of which have been hinted in previous pages. Preferences for playing with certain kinds of probabilities have been demonstrated in the laboratory, and similar preferences for certain odds (long or short, as opposed to midrange) may be observed in betting at race tracks (DaSilva & Dorcus, 1961). Another possibility is that gambling behavior per se is a boughten pleasure, like attending the theatre or a sporting event, where the individual is willing to pay the price of his loss for the diversion it provides. But it is still interesting to question why it is that gambling seems so diverting to so many people; for some, more than diverting, it is enthralling.

An excellent example of such fascination is found in a short novel by Dostoevski, *The Gambler,* which is considered to be autobiographical in theme if not in detail. The protagonist in this work gambled as a communication with destiny, and no amount of mere information was sufficient to inform the player that destiny's message was negative. Two quotations from this work are useful illustrations. The first is a dialog between the gambler and a female gambling partner, Polina. She is speaking:

> "Then you still continue in your conviction that roulette is your only escape and salvation?"
> I answered very earnestly that I did; that as for my confidence that I should win it, it might be absurd; I was ready to admit it.

At a later point, the same woman again questions the gambler's confidence in winning. His reply:

"I am convinced to this moment that I shall win. I confess you have led me now to wonder why my senseless and unseemly failure today has not left the slightest doubt in me. I am still fully convinced that as soon as I begin playing for myself I shall be certain to win."

"Why are you so positive?"

"If you will have it—I don't know. I only know that I *must* win, that is the only resource left me. Well, that's why, perhaps, I fancy I am bound to win."

The suggestion here is that the values connected with gambling may become so powerful that the normal processes operating to create legitimate expectancies about the outcomes of events are badly distorted. A fascinating suggestion about the nature of the super-values involved in gambling has been developed by Cohen. Based on Tyler's observation that the operations used in gambling (spinning wheels, throwing dice, drawing lots or cards) are basically the same as those used in divination, or fortune-telling, Cohen (1960) suggests that:

A contest between two gamblers is not for them a tussle between blind forces of chance, but a struggle between their respective destinies. 'Which of them stands in higher favor with the powers that be?' is the decisive question. For those who think in this fashion, a game of chance or, indeed, any unpredictable event, is a way of knowing whether they are in favor or disfavor with the gods. Hence the wish to have one's fortune told, which yields a clue to one's standing with the gods. The more uncertain and hazardous one's life, the more urgent it is to consult the supernatural powers. (p. 58)

From these speculations emerge some hypotheses about gambling that deserve further study. First, individuals in a precarious condition—financially, socially, or perhaps physically—should be more prone to gamble. They should be willing to pay more and more in the attempt to influence the forces that control destiny to yield a positive response. Second, it should also be the case that the winning and losing of a given amount of money is quite assymetrical in utility, with occasional winnings meaning far more to the subject than more frequent losses and with a concomitant distortion in the memory of past series of winnings and losses. Furthermore, the amount of money possessed by the gambler at any point in time should be quite inconsequential to the desire to gamble. Whether broke or plush, it may be necessary to consult the gods at the gaming tables.

However, although these ideas apply to the case of the habitual and consistently losing gambler, they do not apply to the businessmen who run gambling casinos. Neither is this description appropriate to the occasional tourist or "social gambler." The social development of habitual gamblers forms an intriguing subject for investigation, but one for which reliable data are scarce.

If the extra-monetary values described above are really operative in gambling, then the point is supported that apparently irrational acts are compatible with the activities of men who are considered normal. For worship according to approved conventions is also an attempt to gain the same assurance of divine beneficence; it is possible that similar principles operate to produce the apparent nonmaximization paradoxes mentioned in Chapter IV. "For what shall a man be profited if he shall gain the whole world, and forfeit his life?" (Matthew 16:26)

To return to our discussion at the beginning of this section, the disadvantage of complete certainty is that the opportunity is thereby removed for man to communicate with the forces of determination—for him to "try his luck." Thus, in a sense, superstitions, gambling, and other forms of consultation with the repositories of chance and uncertainty (such as worship) may be seen as attempts of man to learn about his own nature—to establish whether he is doomed or saved, a child of God or a divine reject, a free creature or a servile mechanism. Thus we encounter again the specifically human capacity for self-reflection (the decisive difference between behavior at Stages 5 and 6 as described in Chapter IV). If man is not the only superstitious, gambling, and worshiping animal, he must qualify at least as the only animal for whom these activities are of such paramount importance.

BELIEFS AND THE IDENTIFICATION AND EVALUATION OF SELF

Beliefs that relate the self to various aspects of the external world have evident evaluative significance; such beliefs can be thought of as connections between an otherwise undefined self and real or imagined reference points outside the self. One discovers, or comes to believe, that one is a man or a woman, the offspring of a particular set of parents, a citizen of a particular nation, a relative of other people, and a descendent of apes. Other discoveries are made and adopted into the definition of self: certain foods are good for eating, certain objects are movable by physical force, doorknobs may be turned to open doors, washing with soap removes dirt, and so on. For each object or event that a person conceives, the implicit question arises, "How am I related to that?" or "What is that to me?" The production of rain is no more essential to the ultimate nature of clouds than any of their other properties. In man's view, however, clouds are essentially rainmakers, for it is this property which relates the cloud to the man.

Sarbin (1964) has introduced a set of distinctions regarding the ecological subsystems in which man lives; subecologies are distinguished according to the kinds of functions that relate man to the rest of the world. For example, there is a "self-maintenance ecology," which consists of all those aspects of the external world which a person considers to be relevant to the functions of eating, eliminating waste products, keeping physically healthy, safe, and warm. The "social ecology" includes those objects, usually persons, having social relevance of some kind for the person. The social ecology may be organized cognitively by a set of dimensions—such as relative or nonrelative, threatening or not threatening, known previously or unknown, "above me" or "below me" in social status, and so forth. Similarly, the physical ecology may be organized by a set of cognitive dimensions that result from the nature of the external world, from the perceptual capacities of the person, and from the functional requirements of the person with respect to the physical world. In each case, the array of beliefs that develops with reference to each subecology informs the person of his own identity in that subecology. In this manner effective behavior in that subecology is made possible. Nonveridical beliefs—expectancies that do not match their external counterparts—result in maladaptive or inefficient behavior. Failure to make correct distinctions between poisonous and safe foods, dangerous and friendly people, passable and unpassable roads may be due either to faulty beliefs about the way the world is put together, or to breakdowns in normally reliable ecological relationships. Such breakdowns may be brought about by conditions such as the mislabeling of poisons, disguises of the enemy, or the removal of detour signs.

The ease with which normal ecological relationships—such as those between label (appearance) and contents—can be disturbed by manipulation is the basis for the enormous catalog of human deception and treachery. A sportsman catches fish by concealing a hook in bait of ordinary appearance. Fish can, however, revise their expectations of the relation of appearance to content, thereby increasing their chances of survival. While such "cynicism" makes the sport more difficult for the fisherman, it also imposes additional discriminative requirements upon the fish.

The success of magic shows is based on the same principle as catching fish. Magic as such is not interesting without an understanding of the ordinary organization of the physical ecology: heavy objects will fall if not supported, a rabbit does not hide in an empty hat, most boxes do not have false bottoms, most people have little more than arms up their sleeves, and so forth. The skillful magician capitalizes on these perfectly reasonable beliefs, modifying reality while maintaining the surface appearance that everything is ordinary.

In experiments with human subjects, most psychologists attempt similar alterations, relying on the common expectation in their subjects that what an apparently respectable person tells them about the purpose of a procedure can be believed. Unfortunately, most psychologists are awkward magicians or else they misjudge the cynicism of their clients. There is good evidence that many subjects are not prepared to believe the explanation of the psychologist about the purpose of the experiment (Orne, 1962). This is one reason why children or college undergraduates are preferred as subjects—on the expectation that they have not yet lost their innocent faith in the fidelity of human communication.

For the subecologies discussed above, we can clearly verify the correspondence of beliefs and reality. But it has been repeatedly noted in the foregoing pages that many human beliefs are of the type that cannot be either confirmed or rejected on the basis of available data about the real world. Sarbin (1964) has referred to a special subecology that seems to provide the target for many such beliefs: the "cosmological ecology." Many of the questions that man can put to himself about himself are both reasonable and important. How did I, as man, evolve? What are the limits of space and time? How am I related to the universe? Do I have a "destiny"? What controls my thoughts? The potential evaluative significance of answers to these questions is enormous, paling to insignificance those questions pertaining to the minor subecologies.

We have seen how man can perform the kinds of tricks represented by fishhooks, baggy sleeves, and misleading instructions with reference to the social, physical, and self-maintenance subecologies. What kinds of hoaxes are possible on the cosmological level, where any representation of the "way things are" is a guess, and where the persuasive leverage provided by values is so much greater?

The vast storehouse that anthropologists have accumulated—supernatural beliefs, mysticisms, faiths, creeds, religions, as well as a more modern collection of "scientific" guesses about the cosmos—provides the analog to the magician's bag of tricks. These are the devices man has created to solve the problem which the evolution of his mind necessitates but for which nature has left him no other tools but his mind. The scholar, inspecting the variety and extent of this stockpile, may decide that the best course is "resignation" from the cosmological ecology. There is a psychological price for such cynicism, however, for it is tantamount to the admission that man is a cosmological nonentity. The philosopher can perhaps escape a dilemma by labeling it meaningless, but it is hardly as easy to evade a real psychological dilemma.

Comte urged the thinkers of his day to dispense with useless quibbling over theology and metaphysics and to proceed with the business of positivistic inquiry. Hume, in dealing a blow to idealism, exhorted his readers to "commit to the flames" all matters that did not concern reasonings about either facts or matters of quantity, that is, to confine their attention to ecological subsystems other than the cosmological. But is the person who is deeply puzzled about issues such as his origins and destiny, the freedom of his will, the existence of his soul, or the salvation of it if he decides he has one, or the existence of good and evil, or of God—is such a person to be satisfied with exhortations to "clean up" his thinking? It is doubtful. Rather, the real psychological relevance of these belief options must be recognized where they exist. Psychological consideration of beliefs that are out of bounds for the philosopher is justified if the issues or propositions which those beliefs concern are matters about which people find themselves thinking, and if those beliefs have some behavioral relevance. Only in this manner may psychology be extended to include those individuals living in purely imaginary worlds, and also to the rest of us, whose worlds—it is to be hoped—are less purely imaginary.

In *Reason in Religion,* Santayana (1954) seems to identify man's cosmological curiosity with his immaturity:

> Man is still in his childhood; for he cannot respect an ideal which is not imposed on him against his will, nor can he find satisfaction in a good created by his own action. He is afraid of a universe that leaves him alone. Freedom appalls him; he can apprehend in it nothing but tedium and desolation, so immature is he and so barren does he think himself to be. He has to imagine what the angels would say, so that his own good impulses (which create those angels) may gain in authority, and none of the dangers that surround his poor life make the least impression upon him until he hears that there are hobgoblins hiding in the wood. His moral life, to take shape at all, must appear to him in fantastic symbols. The history of these symbols is therefore the history of his soul. (pp. 222–223)

And yet it is plain that Santayana does not reject the legitimacy of wonder. He suffered no illusions about the finality of positive knowledge as opposed to man's "spiritual illusions."

> Those who think of the truth as the sum of what we read in the newspapers or may find in the Encyclopedia Britannica move sanely enough at one conventional level. Such reports are not ordinarily false. They designate real events, objects truly discoverable on the scale of the human senses; and they trace the relations of these objects and events on the plane of human action. But the form thus assumed by those facts is a mere image. In their aspect and individuality our ideas are signs, not portions, of what exists beyond us; and it is only when experiment and calculation succeed in penetrating beneath the image, that (for instance, in mathematical physics) we may gain some more precise, although still symbolic, notion of the forces that surround us. We and our knowledge are a part of nature; it is therefore inevitable that the rest of nature, in in its concreteness, should be external to us. We cannot share the full reality that other events carry with them. Absolute truth is hidden from us, and the deeper our science goes, the more ghostly it becomes. In entering that temple we have passed out of the sunlight. We are no longer surrounded by living objects, but by the images of the gods. (1964, p. 21)

In passing from the sunlight of comfortable facts, there is a variety of temples we might enter—and a variety of symbols that we might encounter there, containing deeper but more ghostly (cosmological) truths. A testimony to the psychological value of mysteries of this sort is provided in Jung's (1963) autobiography, from which the following is taken:

> It is important to have a secret, a premonition of things unknown. It fills life with something impersonal, a *numinosum*. A man who has never experienced that has missed something important. He must sense that he lives in a world which in some respects is mysterious; that things happen and can be experienced which remain inexplicable; that not everything that happens can be anticipated. The unexpected and the incredible belong in this world. Only then is life whole. For me the world has from the beginning been infinite and ungraspable. (p. 356)

Again, we should emphasize that the reference to mystery in these quotations does not mean they are beyond the bounds of psychological analysis. It is not a legitimate psychological problem to consider whether beliefs about the mysteriousness of nature are true or false, but it is of the highest relevance to consider how these imaginings of the realities behind appearances contribute to psychological functionings. The question of whether muses really exist is hardly as interesting as the question of whether the poet or artist could function without believing in his muse at some level. Even Freud, whose agnosticism, skepticism, and pessimism contrast so sharply with Jung's transcendent and optimistic faith, was driven by a sense of "divine" mission (see Fromm, 1959) and entertained fantastic beliefs in the cosmic meaning of certain signs (especially numbers, see Jones, 1955, Chapter 16).

Santayana would seem to be correct in stating that man is not content to live in the mundane world presented to him by his senses. To give his life cosmic meaning, man engages in a creative scrutiny of the gap between the given facts. James was being descriptive in his essay on the "Will to believe," when he denied the possibility that man *could* be as skeptical as his critical reason might direct him to be. As a result, man's more crucial hopes and fears are based more upon the unseen than the seen. The psychologist must seek to understand how this can work to good or ill.

SUMMARY

This chapter attempts to draw a common strand through a rather diverse array of items—mental illness, anomie and alienation, political deviations and revolutions, gambling, superstitions, and beliefs of various orders (including the cosmological) as they relate to the important psychological task of self-definition. These topics pertain only to human society not to the rest of the animal kingdom, and the quality of self-reflection discussed previously is assumed to be basis for this distinction. Because man submits himself and the world about him to a prodigious and imaginative curiosity, he brings upon himself many problems that could be avoided if he were content to live as a simpler being.

The more important things about a man, as James remarked, are his "ideals and over-beliefs," and these are not likely to be very obviously grounded in his common experience. But as a product of these "ideals and over-beliefs," man has developed art, religion, a creative literature, philosophy, and most certainly, science. The enormous complexity and the endless diversity of cultural products—artifacts, creeds, and ethics— are witness to the vital liberty of man to create his own psychological environment and to attempt the transmission of certain features of that environment to future generations.

But in the process of rule-making and value-judging, man imposes limits on the behavior of those living in a society; some individuals may be regarded as "dangerous" or "mentally ill" because of these conventions. Anomie, alienation, and the desire for political change and revolution are based upon competition among created social norms.

If ideals and over-beliefs are clearly distinguished in the political arena, they are perhaps more open to analysis in the gambling salon or at a voodoo ceremony. We have seen that gambling behavior and superstitions have a common psychological basis in the lack of confidence and uncertainty associated with these experiences. We do not assume that everyone is superstitious or that everyone engages in gambling behavior for the same reasons. Superstitions may be due either to lack of information about cause-effect relationships for highly valued options or, alternatively, to *mis*information. Gambling may stem from a mistakenly high expectation of the possibility of winning *or* from a specific utility of the gambling process itself. For the habitual gambler, the gambling process may assume the significance of a confrontation with destiny. Hence, gambling may have a nonmonetary value that is great enough to impede the correct processing of information. Thus, gambling may be viewed as a kind of primitive religion—the comparison originating in the common objective of these two specifically human enterprises to provide the actor with a means of relating himself to unseen but powerful forces.

Beliefs are like ties created between internal curiosities and the responses of the external world. Thus is the person defined. This works smoothly and logically enough in the spheres of self-maintenance, social life, and physical mobility. But beliefs are also demanded in cosmological matters, and these have the highest evaluative significance of all, legitimating the behavior of martyrs and heroes, and making possible the reversal of the commonly accepted scale of human values. Psychology must seek to develop a better understanding of the workings of these processes.

REFERENCES

Adams, J. K., & Adams, P. A. Realism of confidence judgments. *Psychological Review*, 1961, **68**, 33–45.

Adorno, T. W., Frenkel-Brunswik, E., Levinson, D. J., & Sanford, R. N. *The authoritarian personality*. New York: Harper & Row, 1950.

Allen, V. L. Role theory and consistency theory. In R. P. Abelson, E. Aronson, W. J. McGuire, T. M. Newcomb, M. J. Rosenberg, & P. M. Tannenbaum (Eds.), *Theories of cognitive consistency: A sourcebook*. New York: Rand McNally, 1968.

Allport, F. H. *Social psychology*. Boston: Houghton Mifflin, 1924.

Allport, G. W. Attitudes. In C. Murchison (Ed.), *Handbook of social psychology*. Worcester, Mass.: Clark University Press, 1935.

Allport, G. W. *Personality: A psychological interpretation*. New York: Holt, 1937.

Allport, G. W. The historical background of modern social psychology. In G. Lindzey (Ed.), *Handbook of social psychology*. Vol. 1. Reading, Mass.: Addison-Wesley, 1954.

Allport, G. W., Vernon, P. E., & Lindzey, G. *A study of values: A scale for measuring the dominant interest in personality*. (Rev. ed.) Boston: Houghton Mifflin, 1951.

Asch, S. *Social psychology*. Englewood Cliffs. N.J.: Prentice-Hall, 1952.

Atkinson, J. W. Motivational determinants of risk-taking behavior. *Psychological Review*, 1957, **64**, 359–372.

Atkinson, J. W., Bastian, J. R., Earl, R. W., & Litwin, G. H. The achievement motive, goal setting, and probability preferences. *Journal of Abnormal and Social Psychology*, 1960, **60**, 27–36.

Attneave, F. Psychological probability as a function of experienced frequency. *Journal of Experimental Psychology*, 1953, **46**, 81–86.

Bandura, A. Vicarious processes: A case of no-trial learning. In L. Berkowitz (Ed.), *Advances in experimental social psychology*. Vol. II. New York: Academic Press, 1966.

Bandura, A., & Walters, R. H. *Social learning and personality development*. New York: Holt, Rinehart and Winston, 1963.

Barker, R. G. Explorations in ecological psychology. *American Psychologist*, 1965, **20**, 1–14.

Bateson, G., Jackson, D. D., Haley, J., & Weakland, J. Toward a theory of schizophrenia. *Behavioral Science*, 1956, **1**, 251–264.

Beach, F. A. The descent of instinct, *Psychological Review*, 1955, **62**, 401–410.

Becker, S. W., & Siegel, S. Utility of grades: Level of aspiration in a decision theory context. *Journal of Experimental Psychology*, 1958, **55**, 81–85.

Behan, R. A. Expectancies and Hullian theory. *Psychological Review*, 1953, **60**, 252–256.

Berkowitz, L. The judgmental process in personality functioning. *Psychological Review*, 1960, **67**, 130–142.

Berlyne, D. *Conflict, arousal and curiosity*. New York: McGraw-Hill, 1960.

Block, G. D. Learning in some simple non-biological systems. *The American Scientist*, 1965, **53**, 59–79.

Blum, G. S. *The Blacky pictures, manual of instructions.* New York: Psychological Corporation, 1950.

Boring, E. G. *A history of experimental psychology* (2d ed.) New York: Appleton-Century-Crofts, 1950.

Bronfenbrenner, U. Freudian theories of identification and their derivatives. *Child Development,* 1960, **31,** 15–40.

Bronowski, J. The logic of the mind. *American Scientist,* 1966, **54,** 1–14.

Brown, R. *Social psychology.* New York: Free Press, 1965.

Brozek, J., Guetzkow, H., & Baldwin, M. V. A quantitative study of perception and association in experimental semistarvation. *Journal of Personality,* 1951, **19,** 245–264.

Bruner, J. S. On perceptual readiness. *Psychological Review,* 1957, **64,** 123–152.

Brunswik, E. Probability as a determiner of rat behavior. *Journal of Experimental Psychology,* 1939, **25,** 175–197.

Brunswik, E. *Systematic and representative design of psychological experiments: With results in physical and social perception.* Berkeley: University of California Press, 1947.

Butler, R. A. Discrimination learning by rhesus monkeys to visual-exploration motivation. *Journal of Comparative and Psychological Psychology,* 1953, **46,** 95–98.

Campbell, D. T. Social attitudes and other acquired behavioral dispositions. In S. Koch (Ed.), *Psychology: A study of a science.* Vol. 6. New York: McGraw-Hill, 1963.

Cannon, W. B. *The wisdom of the body.* New York: Norton, 1932.

Cantril, H. *The "why" of man's experience.* New York: Macmillan, 1950.

Cantril, H. *The pattern of human concerns.* New Brunswick, N.J.: Rutgers University Press, 1965.

Cartwright, D. Lewinian theory as a contemporary systematic framework. In S. Koch (Ed.), *Psychology: A study of a science.* Vol. 2. New York: McGraw-Hill, 1959.

Cassirer, E. *An essay on man: An introduction to a philosophy of human culture.* Garden City, N.Y.: Doubleday, 1954.

Chapanis, A. Men, machines, and models. *American Psychologist,* 1961, **16,** 113–131.

Chapanis, N. P., & Chapanis, A. Cognitive dissonance: Five years later. *Psychological Bulletin,* 1964, **61,** 1–22.

Cline, V. B., & Richards, J. M. A factor analytic study of religious belief and behavior. *Journal of Personality and Social Psychology,* 1965, **1,** 569–578.

Cofer, C. N., & Apley, M. H. *Motivation: Theory and research.* New York: Wiley, 1964.

Cohen, J. *Chance, skill, and luck: The psychology of guessing and gambling.* Baltimore: Penguin Books, 1960.

Cohen, J., & Cooper, P. A model for choice in equiprobable situations. *Acta Psychologica,* 1961, **18,** 181–200.

Cohen, J., & Dearnaley, E. J. Skill and judgment of footballers in attempting to score goals. *British Journal of Psychology,* 1962, **53,** 71–88.

Cohen, J., Dearnaley, E. J., & Hansel, C. E. M. The mutual effect of two uncertainties. *Durham Research Review,* 1958a, **2,** 215–222.

Cohen, J., Dearnaley, E. J., & Hansel, C. E. M. Skill and chance: Variations in estimates of skill with an increasing element of chance. *British Journal of Psychology*, 1958b, **49**, 319–323.

Cohen J., & Hansel, C. E. M. *Risk and gambling: The study of subjective probability*. New York: Longmans Green, 1965.

Crandall, V. J., Solomon, D., & Kellaway, R. The value of anticipated events as a determinant of probability learning and extinction. *Journal of General Psychology*, 1958, **58**, 3–10.

Crowne, D. P., & Marlowe, D. *The approval motive: Studies in evaluative dependence*. New York: Wiley, 1964.

Crutchfield, R. C. Conformity and character. *American Psychologist*, 1955, **10**, 191–198.

DaSilva, E. R., & Dorcus, R. M. *Science in betting: The players and the horses*. New York: Harper & Row, 1961.

Deese, J. On the structure of associative meaning. *Psychological Review*, 1962, **69**, 161–175.

Deutsch, J. A., & Jones, A. D. Diluted water: An explanation of the rat's preference for saline. *Journal of Comparative Physiological Psychology*, 1960, **53**, 122–127.

Dobzhansky, T. G. *Mankind evolving, the evolution of the human species*. New Haven, Conn.: Yale University Press, 1962.

Dockeray, F. C., & Valentine, W. L. An analysis of the elementary psychology course at Ohio State University. *Journal of Applied Psychology*, 1935, **19**, 503–520.

Dostoevski, F. *The gambler*. London: Heinemann, 1923.

Duncker, C. On problem-solving. *Psychological Monographs*, 1945, **58**, No. 270, Trans. by L. S. Lees.

Durkheim, E. *Suicide*. 1897, Transl. by J. A. Spaulding & G. Simpson. New York: Free Press, 1958.

Edwards, A. L. *Edwards' personal preference schedule*. New York: Psychological Corporation, 1954.

Edwards, A. L. *The social desirability variable in personality assessment and research*. New York: Dryden, 1957.

Edwards, W. Probability-preferences among bets with differing expected values. *American Journal of Psychology*, 1954, **67**, 56–67.

Edwards, W. The prediction of decisions among bets. *Journal of Experimental Psychology*, 1955, **50**, 201–214.

Edwards, W. Behavioral decision theory. *Annual Review of Psychology*, 1961, **12**, 473–498.

Edwards, W. Utility, subjective probability, their interaction, and variance preferences. *Journal of Conflict Resolution*, 1962, **6**, 42–51.

Edwards, W., Lindman, H., & Phillips, L. D. Emerging technologies for making decisions. In T. M. Newcomb (Ed.), *New Directions in Psychology II*. New York: Holt, Rinehart and Winston, 1965.

Fanon, F. *Wretched of the earth*. New York: Grove Press, 1963.

Feather, N. T. Subjective probability and decision under uncertainty. *Psychological Review*, 1959, **66**, 150–164.

Feather, N. T. Mowrer's revised two factor theory and the motive-expectancy-value model. *Psychological Review*, 1963, **70**, 500–515.

Festinger, L., Riecken, H. W., & Schachter, S. *When prophecy fails.* Minneapolis: University of Minnesota Press, 1956.

Fishbein, M. A consideration of beliefs, attitudes, and their relationships. In I. Steiner and M. Fishbein (Eds.), *Current studies in social psychology.* New York: Holt, Rinehart, and Winston, 1965.

Fishbein, M., & Raven, B. H. The AB scales: An operational definition of belief and attitude. *Human Relations,* 1962, **15,** 35–44.

Frank, J. *Persuasion and healing: A comparative study of psychotherapy.* Baltimore: Johns Hopkins Press, 1961.

Frazer, J. G. *The new golden bough.* T. H. Gaster (Ed.). Garden City, N.Y.: Doubleday, 1961.

Freud, S. *Group psychology and the analysis of the ego.* London: Hogarth, 1921.

Freud, S. *New introductory lectures on psychoanalysis.* New York: Norton, 1933.

Freud, S. *Beyond the pleasure principle.* New York: Liveright, 1950a, Trans. by James Strachey.

Freud, S. Instincts and their vicissitudes. In S. Freud, *Collected papers.* Vol. IV. London: Hogarth, 1950b.

Freud, S. The interpretation of dreams. 1st ed., 1900. In *The complete psychological works of Sigmund Freud,* Vol. IV. London: Hogarth, 1953.

Freud, S., & Bullit, T. *Woodrow Wilson, twenty-eighth president of the United States: A psychological study.* Boston: Houghton Mifflin, 1966.

Freyre, G. *The masters and the slaves.* New York: Knopf, 1956.

Fromm, E. *Sigmund Freud's mission.* New York: Grove Press, 1959.

Galanter, E. The direct measurement of utility and subjective probability. *The American Journal of Psychology,* 1962, **75,** 208–220.

George, A. L., & George, J. L. *Woodrow Wilson and Colonel House: A personality study.* New York: John Day, 1956.

Ghiselli, E. E. *Theory of psychological measurement.* New York: McGraw-Hill, 1964.

Gilliland, A. R. A study of the superstitions of college students. *Journal of Abnormal and Social Psychology,* 1930, **24,** 472–479.

Goffman, E. *Asylums: Essays on the social situation of mental patients and other inmates.* Garden City, N.Y.: Doubleday (Anchor), 1961.

Goffman, E. *Stigma, notes on the management of spoiled identity.* Englewood Cliffs, N.J.: Prentice-Hall, 1963.

Gough, H. G. Clinical versus statistical prediction in psychology. In L. Postman, (Ed.), *Psychology in the making.* New York: Knopf, 1962, 526–584.

Greenberg, J. H. (Ed.) *Universals of language.* (2d ed.) Cambridge, Mass.: MIT Press, 1966.

Greenstein, F. I. Personality and politics: Problems of evidence, inference, and conceptualization. *The American Behavioral Scientist,* 1967, **11,** No. 2, 38–53.

Hall, C. S. *A primer of Freudian psychology.* Cleveland: World Publishing, 1954.

Hall, C. S., & Lindzey, G. *Theories of Personality.* New York: Wiley, 1957.

Handlin, O. Man and magic: Encounters with the machine. *The American Scholar,* 1964, **33,** 408–419.

Hansel, C. E. M. *ESP: A scientific evaluation.* New York: Scribner, 1966.

Hardyck, J. A., & Braden, M. Prophesy fails again: A report of a failure to replicate. *Journal of Abnormal and Social Psychology,* 1962, **65,** 136–141.

Harlow, .H. F. The nature of love. *American Psychologist,* 1958, **13,** 673–685.

Hayes, W. L. *Statistics for psychologists.* New York: Holt, Rinehart and Winston, 1963.

Heath, R. G. Electrical self-stimulation of the brain in man. *American Journal of Psychiatry,* 1963, **120,** 571–577.

Hebb, D. O. Organization of behavior: A neuropsychological theory. New York: Wiley, 1949.

Hebb, D. O. The American revolution. *American Psychologist,* 1960, **15,** 735–745.

Heidbreder, E. *Seven psychologies.* New York: Century Company, 1933.

Heidler, F. Social perception and phenomenal causality. *Psychological Review,* 1944, **51,** 358–374.

Heilbroner, R. L. *The worldly philosophers: The lives, times and ideas of the great economic thinkers.* New York: Simon and Schuster, 1953.

Hersch, P. D., & Scheibe, K. E. Reliability and validity of internal-external control as a personality dimension. *Journal of Consulting Psychology,* 1967, **31,** 609–613.

Hess, R. D., & Shipman, V. C. Maternal influences upon early learning: The cognitive environments of urban pre-school children. In R. D. Hess & R. M. Bear (Eds.), *Early education.* Chicago: Aldine, 1968.

Hoffer, E. *The true believer: Thoughts on the nature of mass movements.* New York: Harper & Row, 1951.

Hofstadter, R. *Social Darwinism in American thought.* (Rev. ed.) Boston: Beacon Press, 1955.

Hollingshead, A. B., & Redlich, F. C. *Social class and mental illness.* New York: Wiley, 1958.

Honigmann, J. J. *Culture and personality.* New York: Harper & Row, 1954.

Hovland, C. I., Janis, I. L., & Kelley, H. H. *Communication and persuasion.* New Haven, Conn.: Yale University Press, 1953.

Hull, C. L. *A behavior system: An introduction to behavior theory concerning the individual organism.* New Haven, Conn.: Yale University Press, 1952.

Hunt, J. M. *Intelligence and experience.* New York: Ronald Press, 1961.

Hyman, H. *Political socialization: A study in the psychology of political behavior.* Glencoe, Ill.: Free Press, 1959.

Irwin, F. W. Relations between value and expectation as mediated by belief in ability to control uncertain events. Paper read at American Psychological Association meetings in Chicago, Ill., 1960.

Irwin, F. W. On desire, aversion, and the affective zero. *Psychological Review,* 1961, **68,** 293–300.

Jackson, J. Structural characteristics of norms. In I. D. Steiner & M. Fishbein (Eds.), *Current studies in social psychology.* New York: Holt, Rinehart and Winston, 1965.

James, W. *Principles of psychology.* New York: Henry Holt, 1890. 2 vols.

Jastrow, J. *Fact and fable in psychology.* New York: Houghton Mifflin, 1900.

Jastrow, J. *The house that Freud built.* New York: Greenberg, 1932.

Jastrow, J. *Wish and wisdom: Episodes in the vagaries of belief.* New York: Appleton-Century, 1935.

Jessor, R. A social learning approach to culture and behavior. In T. Gladwin & W. C. Sturtevant (Eds.), *Anthropology and human behavior.* Washington, D.C.: The Anthropological Society of Washington, 1962.

Jones, E. *The life and work of Sigmund Freud.* Vol. 2. New York: Basic Books, 1955.

Jung, C. G. *Memories, dreams, reflections.* New York: Pantheon Books, 1963.

Katona, G. The relationship between psychology and economics. In S. Koch (Ed.), *Psychology: A study of a science.* Vol. 6. New York: McGraw-Hill, 1963.

Kelly, G. *The psychology of personal constructs.* New York: Norton, 1955. 2 vols.

Kelly, G. A. Man's construction of his alternatives. In G. Lindzey (Ed.), *Assessment of human motives.* New York: Holt, Rinehart and Winston, 1958.

Koch, E. Epilogue. In S. Koch, (Ed.), *Psychology: A study of a science.* Vol. 3. New York: McGraw-Hill, 1959.

Koffka, K. *Principles of Gestalt psychology.* New York: Harcourt, 1935.

Kogan, N., & Wallach, M. A. *Risk taking: A study in cognition and personality.* New York: Holt, Rinehart and Winston, 1964.

Krech, D. Cortical localization of function. In L. Postman (Ed.), *Psychology in the making.* New York: Kropf, 1962. Pp. 31–72.

Krech, D., & Crutchfield, R. S. *Theory and problems of social psychology.* New York: McGraw-Hill, 1948.

Kroger, R. O. The effects of role demands and test-cue properties upon personality test performance. *Journal of Consulting Psychology,* 1967, **31,** 304–312.

Lane, R. E. Political science and psychology. In S. Koch (Ed.), *Psychology: A study of a science.* Vol. 6. New York: McGraw-Hill, 1963.

LaPiere, R. T. Attitudes versus actions. *Social forces,* 1934, **13,** 230–237.

Lasswell, H. D. The structure and function of communication in society. In L. Bryson (Ed.), *The communication of ideas.* New York: Harper & Row, 1948.

Lawrence, D., & Festinger, L. *Deterrents and reinforcement: The psychology of insufficient reward.* Stanford, Calif.: Stanford University Press, 1962.

Lemert, E. M. Paranoia and the dynamics of exclusion. *Sociometry,* 1962, **25,** 2–20.

Lenneberg, E. H. A biological perspective in the study of language. In E. H. Lenneberg, (Ed.), *New directions in the study of language.* Cambridge, Mass.: MIT Press, 1964.

Lenski, G. *The religious factor: A sociological study of religious impact on politics, economics and family.* Garden City, N.Y.: Doubleday, 1961.

Levy, L. H. *Psychological interpretation.* New York: Holt, Rinehart and Winston, 1963.

Lewin, D. *Principles of topological psychology.* New York: McGraw-Hill, 1936.

Lewinsohn, R. *Science, prophecy, and prediction.* New York: Harper & Row, 1961.

Lewis, M. Psychological effect of effort. *Psychological Bulletin,* 1965, **64,** 183–190.

Liebermann, S. The effects of changes in roles on the attitudes of role occupants. *Human Relations,* 1956, **9,** 385–402.

Lifton, R. J. "Thought reform" of Western civilians in Chinese Communist prisons. *Psychiatry,* 1956, **19,** 173–195.

Lindman, H., & Edwards, W. Supplementary report: Unlearning the gambler's fallacy. *Journal of Experimental Psychology,* 1961, **62,** 630.

Lindsley, D. B. Psychophysiology and motivation. In M. R. Jones (Ed.), *Nebraska symposium on motivation: 1957.* Lincoln, Nebr.: University of Nebraska Press, 1957.

Locke, J. Selections from "Essay concerning human understanding." In J. W. Yolton (Ed.), *Theory of knowledge.* New York: Macmillan, 1965.

Logan, F. The Hull-Spence approach. In S. Koch (Ed.), *Psychology: A study of a science.* Vol. 2. New York: McGraw-Hill, 1959.

Luce, R. D, & Raiffa, H. *Games and decisions: Introduction and critical survey.* New York: Wiley, 1957.

Luchins, A. S., & Luchins, E. H. *Rigidity of behavior: A variational approach to the effect of Einstellung.* Eugene, Oreg.: University of Oregon Books, 1959.

Marks, R. W. The effect of probability, desirability, and privilege on the stated expectations of children. *Journal of Personality,* 1951, **19,** 332–351.

Malmo, R. B. Activation: A neuropsychological dimension. *Psychological Review,* 1959, **66,** 367–386.

Maslow, A. H. *Motivation and personality.* New York: Harper & Row, 1954.

McCall, R. J. Invested self-expression: A principle of human motivation. *Psychological Review,* 1963, **70,** 289–303.

McClearn, G. E., & Rodgers, D. A. Genetic factors in alcohol preference of laboratory mice. *Journal of Comparative and Physiological Psychology,* 1961, **54,** 116–119.

McClelland, D. *The achieving society.* Princeton, N.J.: Van Nostrand, 1961.

McDougall, W. *An introduction to social psychology.* London: Methuen, 1908.

Mead, G. H. *Mind, self and society from the standpoint of a social behaviorist.* Chicago: University of Chicago Press, 1934.

Merton, R. K. The self-fulfilling prophecy. *Antioch Review,* 1948, **8,** 193–210.

Merton, R. K. *Social theory and social structure.* Glencoe, Ill: Free Press, 1957.

Merton, R. K. The Matthew effect in science. *Science,* 1968, **159,** 56–63.

Michotte, A. E. *The perception of causality.* London: Methuen, 1963.

Milgram, S. Group pressure and action against a person. *Journal of Abnormal and Social Psychology,* 1964, **69,** 137–143.

Miller, G. A. The magical number seven, plus or minus two: Some limits on our capacity for processing information. *Psychological Review,* 1956, **63,** 81–97.

Miller, G. A. Some psychological studies of grammar. *American Psychologist,* 1962, **17,** 748–762.

Miller, N. E. Liberalization of basic S–R concepts: Extensions to conflict behavior, motivation and social learning. In S. Koch (Ed.), *Psychology: A study of a science.* Vol. 2. New York: McGraw-Hill, 1959.

Miller, N. E., & Dollard, J. *Social learning and imitation.* New Haven, Conn.: Yale University Press, 1941.

Mischel, W., & Grusec, J. E. The model's characteristics as determinants of social learning. *Journal of Personality and Social Psychology,* 1966, **4,** 211–214.

Montgomery, K. C. Exploratory behavior as a function of "similarity" of stimulus situations. *Journal of Comparative and Physiological Psychology,* 1953, **46,** 129–133.

Morse, W. H., & Skinner, B. F. A second type of superstitious behavior in the pigeon. *American Journal of Psychology,* 1957, **70,** 308–311.

Murray, H. A., Barratt, W. G., Homburger, E., *et al. Explorations in personality.* New York: Oxford, 1938.

Murray, H. A. *Thematic apperception test.* Cambridge, Mass.: Harvard University Press, 1943.

Mussen, P. Early socialization: Learning and identification. In T. Newcomb (Ed.), *New directions in psychology III.* New York: Holt, Rinehart and Winston, 1967, 51–110.

Myrdal, G. *An American dilemma: The Negro problem and modern democracy.* New York: Harper & Row, 1944.

Newell, A., Shaw, J. C., & Simon, H. A. Elements of a theory of human problem solving. *Psychological Review,* 1958, **65,** 151–166.

Newell, A., & Simon, H. A. GPS, a program that simulates human thought. In E. Feigenbaum & J. Feldman (Eds.), *Computers and thought.* New York: McGraw-Hill, 1963.

Office of Education. *Earned Degrees Conferred 1965–1966.* Washington, D.C.: U.S. Government Printing Office, 1968.

Olds, J. Physiological mechanisms of reward. In M. R. Jones (Ed.), *Nebraska Symposium on Motivation: 1955.* Lincoln, Nebr.: University of Nebraska Press, 1955.

Orne, M. T. The nature of hypnosis: Artifact and essence. *Journal of Abnormal and Social Psychology,* 1959, **58,** 277–299.

Orne, M. T. On the social psychology of the psychological experiment: With particular reference to demand characteristics and their implications. *American Psychologist,* 1962, **17,** 776–783.

Orne, M. T., & Evans, F. J. Social control in the psychological experiment: Antisocial behavior and hypnosis. *Journal of Personality and Social Psychology,* 1965, **1,** 189–200.

Orne, M. T., & Scheibe, K. E. The contribution of nondeprivation factors in the production of sensory deprivation effect: The psychology of the "panic button." *Journal of Abnormal and Social Psychology,* 1964, **68,** 3–12.

Osgood, C. E. Language universals and psycholinguistics. In J. H. Greenberg

(Ed.), *Universals of language.* (2d ed.) Cambridge, Mass.: MIT Press, 1966.

Osgood, C. E., Suci, G. J., & Tannenbaum, P. H. *The measurement of meaning.* Urbana, Ill.: University of Illinois Press, 1957.

Peters, R. S. *The concept of motivation.* London: Routledge, 1958.

Pfuetze, P. E. *Self, society, existence: Human nature and dialogue in the thought of George Herbert Mead and Martin Buber.* New York: Harper & Row, 1961.

Piaget, J. *The moral judgment of the child.* London: Routledge, 1950.

Piaget, J. *The construction of reality in the child.* New York: Basic Books, 1954.

Piaget, J. *The language and thought of the child.* Cleveland: World Publishing, 1955.

Pierson, D. *Negroes in Brazil.* Carbondale, Ill.: Southern University Press, 1967.

Rachman, D. *Critical essays on psychoanalysis.* New York: Pergamon, 1963.

Rapaport, A. *Fights, games, and debates.* Ann Arbor, Mich.: University of Michigan Press, 1960.

Ritchie, B. Concerning an incurable vagueness in psychological theories. In B. B. Wolman & E. Nagle (Eds.), *Scientific psychology: Principles and approaches.* New York: Basic Books, 1965.

Rogler, L. H., & Hollingshead, A. B. The Puerto Rican spiritualist as a psychiatrist. *American Journal of Sociology,* 1961, **67,** 17–21.

Rokeach, M. *The open and closed mind: Investigations into the nature of belief systems and personality systems.* New York: Basic Books, 1960.

Rokeach, M. *Beliefs, attitudes, and values.* San Francisco: Jossey-Bass, 1968.

Rosenthal, R. Experimenter outcome-orientation and the results of the psychological experiment. *Psychological Bulletin,* 1964, **61,** 405–412.

Rosenthal, R., & Jacobson, L. *Pygmalion in the classroom: Self-fulfilling prophecies and teacher expectations.* New York: Holt, Rinehart, and Winston, 1968.

Rosenzweig, M. R. The mechanisms of hunger and thirst. In L. Postman (Ed.), *Psychology in the making.* New York: Knopf, 1962.

Rotter, J. B. *Social learning and clinical psychology.* Englewood Cliffs, N.J.: Prentice-Hall, 1954.

Rotter, J. B. A historical and theoretical analysis of some broad trends in clinical psychology. In S. Koch (Ed.), *Psychology: A study of a science.* Vol. 5. New York: McGraw-Hill, 1963.

Rotter, J. B. Generalized expectancies for internal versus external control of reinforcement. *Psychological Monographs,* 1966, **80,** No. 609.

Rotter, J. B., Seeman, M., & Liverant, S. Internal versus external control of reinforcements: A major variable in behavior theory. In N. F. Washburn (Ed.), *Decisions, values and groups.* New York: Pergamon Press, 1962.

Royce, J. *The religious aspect of philosophy: A critique of the bases of conduct and of faith.* New York: Houghton Mifflin, 1894.

Russell, B. *Human knowledge: Its scope and limits.* New York: Simon and Schuster, 1948.

Ryle, G. *The concept of mind.* New York: Barnes & Noble, 1949.

Santayana, G. *The life of reason.* (One volume edition.) New York: Scribners, 1954.

Santayana, G. Spirit in the sanctuary. *The American Scholar,* 1964, **33,** 21–26.

Santos, J. F. A psychologist reflects on Brazil and Brazilians. In E. N. Baklanhoff (Ed.), *New perspectives of Brazil,* Nashville, Tenn.: Vanderbilt University Press, 1966.

Sarbin, T. R. The logic of prediction in psychology. *Psychological Review,* 1944, **51,** 210–228.

Sarbin, T. R. Role theory. In G. Lindzey (Ed.), *Handbook of social psychology.* Chap. 6. Vol. 1. Cambridge, Mass.: Addison-Wesley, 1954.

Sarbin, T. R. Anxiety: Reification of a metaphor. *Archives of general psychiatry,* 1964, **10,** 630–638.

Sarbin, T. R. The concept of hallucination. *Journal of Personality,* 1967a, **35,** 359–380.

Sarbin, T. R. On the futility of the proposition that some people be labelled "mentally ill." *Journal of Consulting Psychology,* 1967b, **31,** 447–453.

Sarbin, T. R., & Allen, V. L. Role theory. In G. Lindzey & E. Aronson (Eds.), *Handbook of social psychology.* Chap. 7. Vol. I. (Rev. ed.) Cambridge, Mass.: Addison-Wesley, 1968.

Sarbin, T. R., Scheibe, K. E., & Kroger, R. O. Transformation of social identity. Unpublished manuscript, University of California, Berkeley, 1965.

Sarbin, T. R., Taft, R., & Bailey, D. E. *Clinical inference and cognitive theory.* New York: Holt, Rinehart, and Winston, 1960.

Savage, L. J. *The foundations of statistics.* New York: Wiley, 1954.

Scheibe, K. E. On the relationship between beliefs and values: An experimental and theoretical analysis. Unpublished doctoral dissertation, University of California, Berkeley, 1963.

Scheibe, K. E. The effect of value on statements of expectancy under four experimental conditions. *Psychological Record,* 1964, **14,** 137–144.

Scheibe, K. E., & Sarbin, T. R. Towards a theoretical conceptualization of superstition. *British Journal for the Philosophy of Science,* 1965, **62,** 143–158.

Schein, E. H. The Chinese indoctrination program for prisoners of war. *Psychiatry,* 1956, **19,** 149–172.

Scott, W. A. *Values and organizations: A study of fraternities and sororities.* Skokie, Ill.: Rand McNally, 1965.

Sears, R. R., Maccoby, E. E., & Levin, H. *Patterns of child rearing.* Evanston, Ill.: Row, Peterson & Company, 1957.

Seward, J. P. The structure of functional autonomy. *American Psychologist,* 1963, **18,** 703–710.

Shaver, P. R., & Scheibe, K. E. Transformation of social identity: A study of chronic mental patients and college volunteers in a summer camp setting. *Journal of Psychology,* 1967, **66,** 19–37.

Shepard, O. *The lore of the unicorn.* Boston: Houghton Mifflin, 1930.

Sherif, M. Social psychology: Problems and trends in interdisciplinary relationships. In S. Koch (Ed.), *Psychology: A study of a science.* Vol. 6. New York: McGraw-Hill, 1963.

Siegel, S. A method for obtaining an ordered metric scale. *Psychometrika*, 1956, **21**, 207–216.

Siegel, S. *Choice, strategy, and utility.* New York: McGraw-Hill, 1964.

Simon, H. A. Rational choice and the structure of the environment. *Psychological Review*, 1956, **63**, 129–138.

Simon, H. A. Economics and psychology. In S. Koch (Ed.), *Psychology: A study of a science.* Vol. 6. New York: McGraw-Hill, 1963.

Skinner, B. F. Superstition in the pigeon. *Journal of Experimental Psychology.* 1948, **38**, 168–172.

Smith, L. P. *The English language.* New York: Henry Holt, 1912.

Spencer, H. *The principles of psychology.* New York: Appleton, 1873.

Spranger, E. *Types of men: The psychology and ethics of personality.* Halle: Niemeyer, 1928.

Strong, E. K. *Vocational interests 18 years after college.* Minneapolis: University of Minnesota Press, 1955.

Szasz, T. *The myth of mental illness: Foundations of a theory of personal conduct.* New York: Hoeber-Harper, 1961.

Talbot, E., Miller, S. C., & White, R. B. Some antitherapeutic side effects of hospitalization and psychotherapy. *Psychiatry*, 1964, **27**, 170–176.

Thompson, W. R. Some problems in the genetic study of personality and intelligence. In J. Hirsch (Ed.), *Behavior genetic analysis.* New York: McGraw-Hill, 1967.

Thorp, E. O. *Beat the dealer.* New York: Blaisdell, 1962.

Tolman, E. C. *Purposive behavior in animals and man.* New York: Century Company, 1932.

Tolman, E. C. A psychological model. In T. Parsons & E. A. Shils (Eds.), *Toward a general theory of action.* Cambridge, Mass.: Harvard University Press, 1952.

Tolman, E. C. Principles of purposive behavior. In S. Koch (Ed.), *Psychology: A study of a science.* Vol. 2. New York: McGraw-Hill, 1959.

Tolman, E. C., & Brunswik, E. The organism and the causal texture of the environment. *Psychological Review*, 1935, **42**, 43–77.

Turing, A. M. Can a machine think? In E. A. Feigenbaum & J. Feldman (Eds.), *Computers and thought.* New York: McGraw-Hill, 1963.

Underwood, B. J. *Experimental psychology.* (2d ed.) New York: Appleton-Century-Crofts, 1966.

von Neumann, J., & Morgenstern, O. *Theory of games and economic behavior.* (2d ed.) Princeton, N.J.: Princeton University Press, 1947.

Watson, J. B. Psychology as the behaviorist views it. *Psychological Review*, 1913, **20**, 158–177.

Watson, J. B. Experimental studies on the growth of the emotions. In C. Murchison (Ed.), *Psychologies of 1925.* Worcester, Mass.: Clark University Press, 1928.

Weinberg, S. K. *The sociology of mental disorders.* Chicago: Aldine, 1967.

White, R. W. Motivation reconsidered: The concept of competence. *Psychological Review*, 1959, **66**, 297–333.

Whitehead, A. N. *The aims of education and other essays.* New York: Macmillan, 1929.

Whorf, B. L. *Language, thought and reality*. J. B. Carroll (Ed.), Cambridge, Mass.: MIT Press, 1956.

Wiener, N. *God and golem: A comment on certain points where cybernetics impinges on religion*. Cambridge, Mass.: MIT Press, 1964.

Wolff, J. B. Effectiveness of token rewards for chimpanzees. *Comparative Psychology Monographs*, 1936, **12**, No. 60.

Wolins, L. Responsibility for raw data. *American Psychologist*, 1962, **17**, 657–658.

Woodward, M. The role of low intelligence in delinquency. *British Journal of Delinquency*, 1955, **5**, 281–303.

Young, P. T. The role of hedonic processes in motivation. In M. R. Jones (Ed.), *The Nebraska symposium on motivation: 1955*. Lincoln, Nebr.: University of Nebraska Press, 1955.

Zajonc, R. B. The concepts of balance, congruity and dissonance. *Public Opinion Quarterly*, 1960, **24**, 280–296.

NAME INDEX

Adams, J. K., 38
Adams, P. A., 38
Adler, A., 60
Adorno, T. W., 19, 71
Albertus Magnus, 7
Allen, V. L., 71, 77, 78
Allport, F. H., 18
Allport, G. W., 49, 50, 53, 60, 70
Apley, M. H., 88
Aquinas, St. Thomas, 7
Aristotle, 5, 26–27
Asch, S., 19, 39
Atkinson, J. W., 69, 70, 72, 104, 105
Attneave, F., 37

Bailey, D. E., 30, 36, 87, 125
Baldwin, M. V., 47
Bandura, A., 95, 110
Barker, R. G., 118
Bastian, J. R., 104
Bateson, G., 117
Beach, F. A., 7, 51
Becker, S. W., 58
Behan, R. A., 69
Bentham, Jeremy, 7

Berkowitz, L., 92
Berlyne, D., 54
Bernoulli, D., 57
Block, G. D., 80
Blum, G. S., 50
Boring, E. G., 6, 9, 49, 50
Braden, M., 92
Bronowski, J., 81
Brown, R., 92
Brozek, J., 47
Bruner, J. S., 32
Brunswik, E., 16, 17, 25, 27, 30
Bullit, T., 121
Butler, R. A., 55

Campbell, D. T., 35, 69
Cannon, W. B., 24, 53
Cantril, H., 30, 94, 122, 127
Carroll, L., 22
Cartwright, D., 14
Cassirer, E., 31, 81
Chapanis, A., 78, 92
Chapanis, N. P., 92
Cofer, C. N., 88

151

SUBJECT INDEX